# Hooked

## Legendary Fresh and Saltwater Fish to Catch in a Lifetime

JERRY AUDET

ROCK
POINT

First published in 2025 by Rock Point, an imprint of The Quarto Group,
142 West 36th Street, 4th Floor, New York, NY 10018, USA
(212) 779-4972  www.Quarto.com

Rock Point titles are also available at discount for retail, wholesale,
promotional, and bulk purchase. For details, contact the Special Sales
Manager by email at specialsales@quarto.com or by mail at The Quarto
Group, Attn: Special Sales Manager, 100 Cummings Center Suite 265D,
Beverly, MA 01915 USA.

10 9 8 7 6 5 4 3 2 1

ISBN: 978-1-57715-508-9

Digital edition published in 2025
eISBN: 978-0-7603-9493-9

Library of Congress Control Number: 2024917989

Group Publisher: Rage Kindelsperger
Editorial Director: Erin Canning
Creative Director: Laura Drew
Managing Editor: Cara Donaldson
Editor: Nicole James
Cover Design: Beth Middleworth
Interior Design: Kegley Design and Beth Middleworth

Printed in China

FOR POP. THANK YOU FOR THE GIFT OF FISHING.

# CONTENTS

# SALTWATER

### INSHORE

### OFFSHORE

# INTRODUCTION

## "WHAT MAKES ONE FISH BETTER THAN ANOTHER?"

I was asked that question about 15 years ago at an office barbeque. At first, I laughed, and then awkwardly apologized as the person looked taken aback, insulted, and confused by my reaction. I vividly remember attempting to explain that their question wasn't silly or stupid; it was just very hard and complicated to answer. Not one to shirk from a challenge (or miss an opportunity to talk about fishing), I launched into a long-winded and circuitous answer. I found myself tripping over the explanation, trying first to portray why fishing is so fulfilling, which was relevant, but not focused on the primary question. Then, realizing how far I had wandered off the original path, I started listing the factors that make a fish fun to catch, counting on my fingers as I went, as well as why some of these traits are "better" than others. I discovered, very quickly, that the explanation I was trying to make was full of holes, hypocrisy, circular logic, and half-baked ideology. I repeated the phrase "I'm sorry, I'm having trouble explaining exactly what I mean" many times.

A few minutes into my impromptu lecture, I could see the other person's eyes had glazed over. While they were nodding politely, it was obvious they were lost. In truth, I felt a little lost too. I decided I better wrap it up, and so I changed the subject, but the question haunted me for the rest of the night.

Besides ruminating on the question for the past decade and a half since it was originally asked, in my quest to answer it, I have been informally interviewing many anglers and friends at all different levels. The answers I have received are astoundingly diverse. For some, what makes a fish "best" is the battle the fish puts up when hooked. It's the "tug is the drug" that makes a fish addicting to pursue and fun to catch. This is why anglers adore fish such as largemouth, carp, marlin, or tarpon—because the fight is always epic, and the fish brawls chaotically with the angler.

Other anglers told me they enjoy catching fish because they are plentiful and provide relentless action for hours on end. Crappie, flounder, and smallmouth all fit this bill—high concentrations of feisty fish that mean nonstop hits and fast-paced, rod-bending action. Then there were anglers on the other side of that coin who confided they live for catching fish that are extremely crafty and wily. Musky, steelhead, and bonefish are great examples of species that speak to these types of anglers. Catching just a few of these maddeningly tricky fish each season is an accomplishment, and more satisfying for anglers than landing a thousand of a different species.

One explanation I heard many times as to why an angler loved one species over another had to do with where the fish lived—the beauty or excitement of its natural surroundings and the adventures the pursuit of the fish took the angler on. This was a theme that crossed many species—even in cities and urban areas—but the brook trout, yellowfin, and halibut come to mind right away, because they pull anglers into some of the wildest waters in the world. And finally, many, many anglers have told me they simply love one species over another because they can "own it." They're accessible in their local waters and don't require travel or lots of money to pursue—walleye, catfish, and striped bass all qualify as local, deeply satisfying fisheries. Being the local legend, champion, or expert on your local water is a feeling that transcends species or geography.

While we all tend to favor some traits more than others, as you might expect, it's actually a combination of numerous factors that attracts an angler to one fish or another. Even for the same species, the reasons can be as diverse as the anglers themselves. I find it so fascinating that an angler in Idaho can feel as strongly about walleye, as an angler in Florida can feel about snook, as an angler in Europe can feel about pike, or as an angler in Africa can feel about tarpon. These people, and these fish, are all so very different, yet the feeling of devotion and adoration is shared. The feelings we have for the fish we love is a uniting commonality—a language we can all understand, no matter how different our angling pursuits.

These findings, and much thought, led me to an epiphany. I would argue, adamantly, that what makes a fish great isn't its speed, power, or intelligence. Instead, what makes a game fish great is more about who the angler is, than what the fish is. Our appreciation—or infatuation, or obsession—of a specific fish, and fishing in general, is a gut feeling, which is sometimes hard to measure and is as diverse and varied as we are as fishermen and -women. The ultimate devotion we feel to a fish—and fishing for them—transcends a list, spec-sheet, logical argument, or even reason. It's a feeling, not an equation, and as such is part of who we are. The beauty, the value, and the ranking, is, as they say, in the eye of the beholder.

This realization helped inform the list of game fish you will find in these pages. It contains the species that carry with them the highest number of most devoted anglers. These are the fish that speak most strongly and deeply to most of us. These are the fish that are most responsible for forging men and women into lifelong anglers and holding their attention through a lifetime of pursuit. Some are fish we encounter and catch early in our journey, which draw us into the sport. For many, we need look no further, as they are the fish that mean the most to us and easily hold our focus for a lifetime. Other fish we discover and fall in love with much farther along our path as we make our way through the immense world of angling. These "second stage" fish are often the species that really drive the devotion, the obsession, and the passion in an angler's heart. And yet still others on this list are fish we graduate to as we reach the highest levels of knowledge and experience. They are tricky to catch, grow to giant sizes, or are rare to encounter—or some combination of all these traits. Or perhaps none of those things: the world of fishing is immense, and it sometimes simply takes many years and many fish to finally settle on our favorites.

Regardless of what category they fall into for you, the fish within these pages all have something in common: they really matter to the angling community, and we are devoted to them. If you're looking for a new challenge, or want to learn about what's out there, this list is a great place to start. For each fish, I've started with a "level of difficulty" rating system so that you can see what you're in for; I consider 1 or 2 fish for a beginner, and 3 or 4 fish for a more experienced angler. I then include locations which I've called "Perfect Spot." These were chosen to best represent either waters that offer you the best chance of finding numbers or size (or both) of the fish in question, or that represent special or interesting places an angler should put on their "bucket list" if they're particularly passionate about that species. In most cases, the locations represent all of this, and for more than a few, they are also personal favorites. I continue with the preferred habitat of the fish and the ideal season for fishing them. This is followed by a few simple bits of advice about where, when, and how to catch the fish, just enough to set you on your way. Finally, I give you a snapshot of how big a typically sized fish of that species would be, and what is considered a trophy, or a very big fish. At the end of the profile, I've also included the world record size, location, and date for each species, to give perspective on your own catches—and to help you dream big.

One more thing to know about this list—it's not exhaustive. The world of angling is vast, and the number of fish that can be caught is staggering. In North America, there are plenty of fish that didn't make this list and drawing the line was particularly difficult in some cases. Fish like sunfish, perch (including surf perch), pickerel, sheepshead, croaker, corvina, bluefish, grouper, and sheefish represent just some of those examples—and there are plenty of others. To the reader out there who feels particularly passionate about one of these species, or any other that has been left off the list, know that I recognize the omissions. Also know if a fish didn't make this list, it might mean you have something truly special—a secret fish that you know brings you satisfaction and fun, that most others have missed and don't see the potential. Hold onto it!

So then, these fish, as a collective, are chosen because they represent what is most inspiring on every trip and in every season through our entire lives. They are the fish that consume our weekends and our early-morning sunrises. They are the fish that give us trembling hands, weak knees, and a pounding heart. They are the fish of which epic tales are crafted and from which enduring memories are made. These are the fish that keep us up at night dreaming about the "one that got away," and the revenge we seek in the next trip. They are the fish that connect us to the natural world and on which lifelong relationships with both are built. They are the fish that have changed us, and helped make us into the dedicated, passionate, and relentless anglers we are today—both on and off the water.

# FRESHWATER FISH

# BUTTERFLY
# PEACOCK BASS

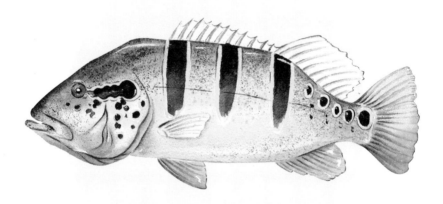

**· 5 POUNDS (2.3 KG) ·**

| | |
|---|---|
| **PERFECT SPOT** | Dade County, Florida, United States |
| **PREFERRED HABITAT** | Butterfly peacock bass need warm water of 75 to 82°F (24 to 28°C) with lots of hiding spots. They prefer structure and slow-moving water, so fishing Florida's many canals is the best bet. |
| **SEASON** | Butterfly peacocks can be caught year-round, but spring (March to May) is considered the best. |
| **TOP TECHNIQUE** | Soft plastics that mimic minnows are a top pick for peacocks, but top water and hard plastic swimmers work very well too. Fly fishermen can catch peacocks with typical bass flies, or smaller saltwater patterns. |
| **AVERAGE SIZE** | 2 to 4 pounds (0.9 to 1.8 kg) |
| **RECORD SIZE LOCATION & DATE** | 12 pounds 9 ounces (6 kg); Chiguano River, Venezuela |

# THE BUTTERFLY PEACOCK BASS IS SO BRIGHTLY COLORED AND

strikingly built that it's a top contender for the most dramatic game fish of them all. They are a bright green across their backs, sunshine yellow on their flanks with jet-black banding, and showcase a highly contrasted fiery orange along their bellies. Their broad and fan-like tail is multicolored, transitioning from green to orange, with a large dark spot similar to a red drum. Their head is huge compared to their bodies, and males have a bulbous nodule at the top, which transitions steeply from the hump to their cavernous mouth. Their eyes are bright red, which completes the ensemble; the kaleidoscope of color makes it obvious where they get their name.

The butterfly peacock is one of the largest of the 9 species of peacock bass and is native to the northeast coast of South America where it can be found in several river systems that course through heavy jungle. That said, they found a new home in the United States when they were introduced to Southeast Florida in 1983. They were stocked in this warm climate in the hopes they would prey on other nuisance species, such as tilapia and oscars. Since then, their population has ballooned. However, biologists have determined that these striking fish not only do not hurt the native fish species but have safely integrated into the natural flora and fauna as pest control and have helped stabilize their new home—a rare case of an introduced species doing more good than harm.

The South Florida population of butterfly peacock has become extremely popular across the world, as it draws many anglers who want to add the peacock to their life list without venturing into more remote areas of South America. Their beauty is stunning, but more astounding is their voracious appetite and ultra-aggressive nature. They're renowned for being even more bullish than largemouth bass and will strike at just about anything that looks even remotely edible. Once hooked, they go berserk and will rip drag before erupting from the surface in multiple leaps and then tail-walk across the surface as if they have wings. They are unrelenting in their fight to free themselves and pound for pound outclass the already mighty largemouth. Peacocks are also known to school-up, and large groups of them will hang over the same spots, all eager to put a deep bend in an angler's rod.

Fishing for peacocks will feel familiar to any angler who has pursued largemouth—all the same principles apply. They primarily feed on other fish, so lures that mimic minnows are very effective, but the peacock isn't fussy and your favorite largemouth lure is likely just as effective. Likewise, the same rods and reels are equally suitable for peacocks, who are similarly sized. While they are found in shallow lakes and ponds in Florida, they are most at home in very warm waters with slow-moving current and lots of structure. As such, they have found a perfectly adoptable home in Florida's labyrinth of canals that crisscross the lower portions of the state. It is thought that today these rainbow-colored fish inhabit at least 300 miles (483 km) of the interconnected canal systems. While much of this urban maze of water is fishable by small boat or kayak, it is particularly beloved by shore based or "bank" anglers. There are so many spots that are easy to access, which can be cast all the way across—making every inch of the peacock's home accessible to anglers on foot. These canals are also typically crystal clear, giving anglers the ability to sight fish easily with both lures and flies—something that can prove particularly rewarding and hilariously fun. Yet, anglers love the butterfly peacocks of Florida just as much for where it takes them: scouting out the best spots and discovering secret nooks and crannies affords a feeling of much-sought-after exploration and adventure.

# CARP

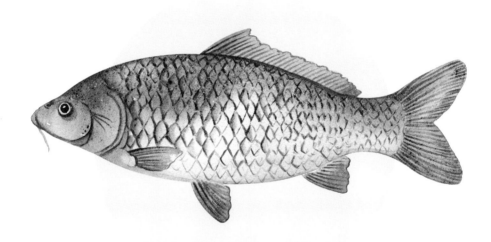

|  | · 40 POUNDS (18 KG) · |
|:---:|:---:|
| **DIFFICULTY** | **TROPHY SIZE** |

| | |
|---:|:---|
| **PERFECT SPOT** | Linear Fisheries, United Kingdom; Connecticut River, United States |
| **PREFERRED HABITAT** | Carp prefer warmer, shallower, slower moving waters with soft bottoms and lots of hiding places but can thrive in a wide range of environments with an optimum water temperature between 70 and 90°F (21 and 32°C). |
| **SEASON** | Carp are caught in spring through fall. |
| **TOP TECHNIQUE** | A baited hook with simple baits such as worms, crayfish, or corn work well to catch carp, but many anglers use area baiting and specially made carp baits to entice fish into their area. Fly fishermen and -women have fallen in love with carp, and small "buggy" patterns work best. |
| **AVERAGE SIZE** | 5 to 25 pounds (2.3 to 11 kg) |
| **RECORD SIZE LOCATION & DATE** | 75 pounds 11 ounces (34 kg); Lac de St. Cassien, France |

## CARP FISHING HAS BEEN POPULAR IN EUROPE FOR AT LEAST

a century and a half and remains one of the top angling pursuits throughout the continent today. In North America, carp fishing has only recently undergone a revolution. The common carp—the most popular species—was introduced to North America in the late 1800s. While initially it had some food value, for much of the nineteenth and twentieth centuries carp were viewed primarily as "trash fish," both on the plate and at the end of a line. Then, with the popularity of fly fishing exploding in the last 40 years, anglers began branching out to try and catch everything and anything with a fly rod, and the carp was "rediscovered." While there were certainly anglers who felt passionate about these rowdy and fickle fish, they have erupted in popularity in this modern age of fly fishing as anglers have dropped their preconceived notions, and now see the carp for the amazing quarry that they are.

Not long after fly anglers fell in love with the carp, they got the nickname "poor man's bonefish," an homage to the mystical saltwater species, which speaks directly to why they are such a fantastic game fish. While you wouldn't expect a large, full-bodied fish that sucks up crayfish in muddy ponds to be similar to a fish that thrives in inches of water over white-sand flats, the comparison is profound: both can be sight-fished, both take similarly patterned and sized flies, both are notoriously skittish, and both rip drag off the reel like a rocket ship. The thing that sets the carp apart—and where the moniker "poor man" comes in—is that these fish are found in so many "ordinary" places that are accessible to anglers of any means. Giant 40 pound (18 kg) carp can be caught in muddy ponds smack dab in the middle of a city park—no need to travel to exotic tropical islands or rely on a guide and a flats skiff to catch carp.

The common carp is deemed ugly by many, and beautiful only by some. They are a deep-bodied fish, often plump and round, and covered with huge scales that overlap like armor. They vary in color from brown to canary yellow and have sizable free-flowing fins and a massive tail that makes them both agile and powerful. The strangest part of the carp's appearance is their face, which is dominated by huge, rubbery, thick lips which open in an "O." They use this "O" mouth to vacuum up food from the bottom, where mud and dirt is filtered in search of insects, crustaceans, and vegetation. On either side of their mouths are barbels, like a goatee, which help in detecting food through taste and touch. Their eyes are big and placed high on the head—many anglers swear they see a sparkle of intelligence in that large pupil that isn't found in other fish.

Carp are notorious for being hard to catch, which is a major component of their allure as game fish. They have excellent senses and are spooked easily by anything foreign in their environment, especially when they're in the shallows. Therefore, even giants over 30 pounds (14 kg) require very small hooks and light leaders, and a highly refined, finessed approach. It's incredible—almost magical—how carp have the ability, somehow, to detect a hook, line, or bait as being dangerous. This is just as often a result of the fish detecting the angler, as opposed to the tackle. As such, most anglers will tell you that the most important part of catching carp is avoiding detection. This is one of the main reasons most anglers fish from shore (the other being that carp like to feed in the shallows). A boat, kayak, or canoe can be intrusive, and if a carp starts to associate the boat with being hooked, their memories are long, and they won't forget. The hyper-focused, shore-based carp angler will go to any lengths to avoid detection—they are known to use hunting blinds and wear camouflage, or even face paint and ghillie suits!

The easiest way to catch carp is through a process of baiting. This isn't legal everywhere, but in many places, anglers will throw feed into the water in which they are fishing, drawing the fish to the general area. Some anglers might do this for days or even weeks leading up to their fishing trip. There are many ways to approach baiting, from simply throwing carp bait in the water to using complicated automatic feeders that release food around the clock. No matter the method, the point is that once the fish are anticipating feed in the area, they are more apt to frequent the spot. On the hook, simple baits such as worms, corn, and bread are very effective, but there is an extensive selection of man-made baits now, specifically designed for carp. That said, many experienced anglers still insist it can be best to fish with bait that is similar to whatever the carp are focused on—giving them bread when they're feeding on berries, for example, is ill advised. Once prepared, in most cases baits are casted out with long, sensitive rods and anglers then wait patiently for carp to be attracted to their offering. Anglers often hide themselves from sight, and use bite alarms—either bells, chimes, or special electronic alarms on the tip of the rod—to alert them to the subtlest bites.

Baiting is the most effective way to catch both high numbers and large sizes, but casting to carp who are feeding naturally is more exciting by all accounts. The anglers attempt to spot feeding carp at a distance is either by spotting their bodies, or the plumes of mud and debris dislodged from the bottom by the fish rooting around for food (this is called "grubbing"). In the same careful manner that a hunter sneaks up on a deer, the angler, seeing the signs of a fish, stalks them slowly and quietly, sometimes for extended periods over considerable distance. Once within range, the angler might settle down and observe for a long time, knowing they may only get a single cast, and if they botch it they end their entire day fishing. They will time it just right, to cast to the fish when their heads are down and vacuuming up feed from the bottom, unaware of motion on the bank. Once the fly, bait, or lure is in position, waiting for the fish to suck it in is the easy part—it's getting the hook set fast enough that's the hard part. Carp are experts at sorting and rejecting anything they don't want and can spit out a hook in a fraction of a second.

Once actually hooked, carp are demons. They will torch a drag, burning off-line, and are crafty enough to take anglers into weeds, wood, and rocks. They have unending endurance, as they are fatigue resistant, being used to very warm, low-oxygen waters. Since anglers typically use light leaders and small hooks to fool the fish, carp also must be fought gingerly and patiently or the line will break. It's nerve wracking fighting a giant carp, and takes some getting used to, but the adrenaline surge that comes with it defines the phrase "the tug is the drug." The whole process—from finding where carp are feeding, to stalking them, to making the perfect cast and finally getting the fish in the net—is one of intense study, preparedness, and nerves of steel. For a fish that is so common and humble, it's an amazing contrast, and one that anyone can experience with a bit of hard work and a healthy measure of stealth.

# CRAPPIE

| | |
|---|---|
| **PERFECT SPOT** | Grenada Lake, Mississippi, United States; St. John's River, Florida, United States |
| **PREFERRED HABITAT** | Crappie prefer heavy structure, such as sunken log piles and dense vegetation. They move around frequently in large schools and go where feed is densest and where water temperatures are between 60 and 75°F (16 and 24°C), though this is highly variable by season and region. |
| **SEASON** | Crappie can be caught year-round, including through ice. They feed best during low-light periods. |
| **TOP TECHNIQUE** | Jigging with soft plastics is very effective, but many anglers prefer using live bait (worm, grub, minnow) under a float. The largest crappie will attack bass lures like crank baits and spinners. |
| **AVERAGE SIZE** | 5 to 8 inches (13 cm to 20 cm) |
| **RECORD SIZE LOCATION & DATE** | Black crappie: 5 pounds 7 ounces (2.5 kg), 19 ¼ inches (49 cm); Tennessee, United States, 2018 |

## CRAPPIE, ALSO KNOWN AS CALICO OR SPECKLED BASS, ARE

one of the most pursued fish in North America (edged out by largemouth bass, which are number one, and tied with walleye and sunfish for numbers two to four). There are a couple of different species, and all are exceedingly popular and incredibly important as "around the corner" fisheries. While they are native to the Eastern and Southern United States, they have been introduced across most of the country and are found throughout much of Mexico and Southern Canada. Crappie are very adaptable fish and can handle a diverse spectrum of calm water conditions, in terms of pH, dissolved oxygen, and temperatures as high as 95°F (35°C), and they can even live in low salinity. This means that they are available to a huge number of anglers, no matter where they live.

For some reason, you don't hear it too often, but crappie are undeniably handsome fish. The black crappie has a striking, checker-like patterning of black and white, with an iridescent overtone of green. The white crappie is similar, though less striking, but lighter overall with more banding and less checkering. Often described as "half sunfish, half bass," crappie are a typical panfish shape, but have large, round mouths— large enough to inhale minnows. Most anglers don't know that crappie are relatively slow growers; while they mature rapidly, it takes at least 4 years to reach 10 inches (25 cm), and depending on the water conditions and available feed, it can take more than 7 years (especially in northern zones).

Though they're "everywhere," crappie aren't just popular because they're common—they're beloved because they're an awesome game fish. Anglers love the combination of fast-paced action and finicky mystery that these feisty panfish provide. They are tightly schooling fish, so once you hook a few, you are likely to catch a pile of them—if they'll bite. Often compared to walleye (for several reasons), crappie can be savage and aggressive one minute—exploding on lures with reckless abandon—and then lock jawed the next. Plus, getting bait into the heavy structure they love can be risky for boats and an easy way to lose a lot of tackle, but that's part of the challenge, and the allure of fishing for them.

No conversation of crappie fishing can pass without mention of how beloved table fare they are. Many anglers cite crappie as their favorite "eating" fish, and catching dinner is very meaningful to these anglers. They feel fiercely connected to the process of the hunt, the catch, and the harvest—it makes crappie fishing deeply personal. But even for the catch and release angler, crappie are a fish that engages them with nature, gets them out on the water, and offers them a chance to hunt local trophies and dial in on their regional waters. It's a fishery the angler can own, and challenge themselves with, through personal achievement and responsible harvest.

Crappie have similar feeding behavior as walleye, preferring dawn, dusk, and total darkness, where they move in schools hunting anything they can snatch up. When it's gotten too dark to tie a knot without a light, that's when crappie really turn on. Despite this, most anglers focus on catching them during the day and look for large concentrations of fish staged in a tight area. Crappie can be caught in all sorts of different ways, but jigging is one of the most popular methods year-round. The best method is using small grubs (live or rubber) on ball head jigs and dropping them down and wiggling them in, over, and around heavy structure, drop-offs, and holes. However, many sharpies will point out that if you want to experience a truly fired-up crappie, or catch a trophy, you should be working small crank baits, spinners, and live bait around the edges of the day—especially at or after sunset during the warmer months. Crappie really transform as the light fades, switching from passive nibblers into savage attackers—and that's when the trophies are landed.

LAKES AND PONDS

# LAKE TROUT

| | |
|---|---|
|  **DIFFICULTY** | **· 40 POUNDS (18 KG) ·** **TROPHY SIZE** |

| | |
|---|---|
| **PERFECT SPOT** | Great Bear Lake, Northwest Territories, Canada; Lake Willoughby, United States |
| **PREFERRED HABITAT** | Lake trout require cold—between 40 and 50°F (4 and 10°C)—clean, highly oxygenated water and cannot survive without all three. Most of the year they will be down deep—50- to 100-plus feet (15.24 m to 30.48 m)—over reefs and humps, where they ambush prey. |
| **SEASON** | There are 2 laker seasons: summer and winter. In summer, lakers are found deep and are often concentrated in small areas. In cold months, they spread out, and come into much shallower water to hunt. |
| **TOP TECHNIQUE** | Most anglers troll for lake trout, either with or without downriggers, targeting areas below the thermocline. Special trolling spoons and spinners are top choices, but deep swimming lures work well. Vertical jigging is an excellent technique on smaller lakes, and ice fishing is one of the top choices for dedicated anglers. |
| **AVERAGE SIZE** | 5 to 20 pounds (2.3 to 9 kg) |
| **RECORD SIZE LOCATION & DATE** | 72 pounds (33 kg); Great Bear Lake, Northwest Territories, Canada |

# LAKE TROUT ARE ANCIENT, MASSIVE, LURKERS OF THE DEEP,

dark places. As their name suggests, these fish are in the trout family, and as such they have a common trout-shaped body—tubular and thick, with a broad, powerful tail. The big difference in their bodies is that they get much, much larger than typical trout. The world record exceeds 70 pounds (32 kg), and it's common for "lakers" to eclipse 30 pounds (1.4 kg)! They're a beautiful, subtly patterned fish, often described as very clean, with flawless, reflective silver-to-green sides that shimmer like polished metal, speckled with a dusting of pure white spots. Because of their size, lakers are apex predators, and they use both stealth and speed to quickly overpower large prey in the deepest parts of typical lakes. They've been known to swallow 10-inch-long (25 cm) perch and 3-pound (1.4 kg) walleye.

Lake trout are also one of the longest-lived freshwater fish. They are most comfortable in large, deep, and consistently cold lakes, where they can always find water between 40 and 50°F (4 and 10°C). In these waters, lakers can live as long as 70 years, and in most places, they easily reach 25 years. They mature and grow extremely slowly, primarily because their oligotrophic homes are low in plant and insect life, due to their great depths, low temperatures, and limited nutrients. Add in that for most of their lives, they live in the dark depths below the thermocline where even less life ventures, and it's easy to see why they grow so slowly and live so long.

Many anglers use downriggers to pursue lakers in the depths. Their creation is mostly credited to laker anglers in the Great Lakes, who came up with the method in the 1950s and '60s. If you're unfamiliar with downriggers, they're an ingenious system that allows an angler to troll a lure (often a spoon or spinner) at a specified, and very deep, depth. The basic concept relies on a small boom arm that controls a heavy weight of about 6 to 15 pounds (2.7 to 7 kg), attached to cable that can be adjusted to a specific depth. A special clip is connected from the weight to the fishing line on the rod, and the weight then holds the lure down where the lakers are. When a fish strikes, it pulls the line off the clip, and the angler fights the fish on the trolling rod, without the weight attached. While the lure on the end of a downrigger setup can be as simple as a short leader and a small spoon, many laker anglers use incredibly complex, flashy lure systems. These involve long trains of fish-attracting blades that flip and spin like a school of bait. Anglers who love trolling for lakers get very specific about their choices and often guard them to keep the best combinations secret.

With or without downriggers, fishing for lake trout can be intimidating for many anglers. The thought of getting a line down 100-plus feet (30 m) is hard for some anglers to wrap their heads around. However, dedicated experts and the laker obsessed will tell you that it doesn't have to be complicated. Particularly on smaller bodies of water, modern fish finders allow anglers to find and set up over the top of fish they mark. Then, typical bass gear can be very effective in vertically jigging for really big lakers. This method is especially productive in the summer, when lakers will congregate in cold-water seeps and deep-water structures. The thump of a laker hitting a falling jig is something that is not replicable with trolling gear, and in that split second before the fish starts to pull, the angler doesn't know whether the fish is 5 or 50 pounds (2.3 to 23 kg)—and that is a very exciting, heart-stopping couple of moments. The thrill can be even more intense when ice fishing for lakers—the tackle is even lighter, the fish come in shallow, and often feed even more aggressively when the water "locks up" in winter—no boat needed whatsoever.

**LAKES AND PONDS**

# LARGEMOUTH BASS

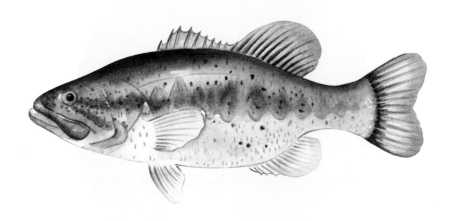

| | |
|---|---|
| **DIFFICULTY** | **· 7 TO 12 POUNDS (3.2 TO 5 KG) ·**<br>**TROPHY SIZE** |

| | |
|---|---|
| **PERFECT SPOT** | Lake Okeechobee, United States; El Salto, Mexico |
| **PREFERRED HABITAT** | Largemouth are structure-oriented fish. They prefer heavy vegetation, fallen trees, docks, and boulders to hide around, and generally stay out of any current. Otherwise, they are adaptable and can be found in diverse warmer waters around the world between 60 and 80°F (16 and 27°C). |
| **SEASON** | Largemouth can be caught year-round, including through the ice, but fishing is best in early spring through fall. |
| **TOP TECHNIQUE** | There is no best way to catch largemouth—it's one of the best things about them—but many anglers would agree that fishing topwater for bass is the most fun. For a trophy-sized fish, huge swimbaits have become more and more popular, but nothing will ever beat big live bait. |
| **AVERAGE SIZE** | 1 to 6 pounds (0.5 to 2.7 kg), region specific |
| **RECORD SIZE LOCATION & DATE** | Two-way tie: 22 pounds 4 ounces (10 kg); Shiga, Japan, 2009; Georgia, United States, 1932 |

## OF ALL THE SPECIES IN THIS BOOK, THE LARGEMOUTH MAY

ultimately be the most beloved and, arguably, the most important to the world of sportfishing. While marlin and tuna are the mightiest, there is no fish that has had more of an impact on more anglers throughout the world than the humble largemouth. While they are native to the Mississippi basin and the Great Lakes of the United States, they are now found on all the continents of the world (except Antarctica), and in a huge number of countries and hundreds of thousands of waterways. They are the perfect game fish for numerous reasons, but the factors that make them truly special boils down to two characteristics.

The first, and likely the most important, is their ferocity and vigor when hooked. Largemouth fight heroically every time on the line, without exception, and no matter their size. Whether you tie into a half-pound juvenile (0.2 kg) or a 14-pound (6 kg) monster, you can count on them giving 100 percent from the second they feel the prickle of the hook point. They are supreme leapers who launch into the air again and again when hooked, and after the initial jumps, they dive and hunt for the bottom like a possessed torpedo. They also prefer heavy vegetation, downed wood, and docks and piers, and are notorious for burying themselves in the structure, attempting to rub the lure off or break the line. This leaves the angler to try and figure out how to untangle them while the bass is still pulling and thrashing with everything it's got. Even if an angler has caught thousands of fish across the globe, there remains a perpetual appreciation for the power and brutishness of the mighty largemouth. In the simplest words: their fight never gets old.

But there is another beloved characteristic of the largemouth, and that is its accessibility. Any angler can pursue this pinnacle gamefish with simple, inexpensive tackle, virtually anywhere there's some freshwater. Smaller fish are eager participants in any angler's pursuit, and concentrations are high enough anyone can expect to catch several fish every trip. The bass is responsible for drawing so many anglers into the sport and is a gateway to many other species and other avenues of angling. Part of this is because even hefty 3- and 4-pound (1.4 to 1.8 kg) largemouth can be caught without spending long hours plying every inch of a pond or lake; it doesn't take a lifetime of learning.

Yet, for those who want to take their fishing to the next level, the largemouth can be that outlet, too. Landing true, trophy-class "lunkers" with consistency takes dedication and patience of the highest degree, as well as keen powers of observation and a methodical nature. It can be frustrating, almost painful at times, trying to keep focus only on the giants, and ignoring the temptation of smaller fish. Anglers who pursue the ultimate, top-tier, trophy-class fish in the 8- to 15-pound (4 to 7 kg) class take fishing unquestionably seriously, and spend inordinate amounts of money, time, and effort in reaching their goals. They stop at nothing, and meticulously obsess over lure types and presentations, weather patterns, the moon phase, bait development, water conditions, and all the other factors that go into getting the real lunkers to strike.

Largemouth are typically some shade of green or olive, with irregular black splotches or banding along their midline. Their thick, heavy bodies are powered by a wide, flowing, triangular tail. Their hallmark is their huge "bucket mouth." This gaping maw is often nearly as big around as the size of their bodies, with the top hinge extending beyond their eye (a key trait that differentiates them from smallmouth bass). Their mouth underlies their voracious nature, and with such a massive, cavernous mouth, that means the bass will try to eat anything that swims, crawls, floats, or scuttles through its aquatic environment. While they prefer to ambush prey and attack over short distances, largemouth are dauntless and bold, and will chase prey with a zeal that reflects their overall nature as the apex predator in their home waters.

Largemouth are surprisingly long lived, able to reach 15 years old in the wild. The growing season is extremely important for how big largemouth will get, and roughly corresponds to the period of time the water stays between 60 and 80°F (16 and 27°C). In some areas of the country—like many of the Southeast states, Texas, and Florida— this can be virtually year-round. In many of these places, bass grow both fast and huge, capable of exceeding 15 pounds in 10 years.

One of the important attributes of the largemouth that often gets lost is its contribution to tackle and lure development over the last two centuries. Many different innovations got started or became embedded with largemouth anglers, many of which have since become vitally important in other freshwater and saltwater angling. From rubber worms and wacky rigging to spinnerbaits and swimbaits, to forward facing sonar and flipping and pitching, there are a dizzying array of inventions, tactics, and techniques that would simply never exist without the wide world of largemouth fishing. Many of these innovations are due to tournament anglers, who are constantly pushing for new technology and tactics to stay ahead of their competitors. Largemouth tournaments are big money, with millions of dollars in prizes and sponsorship deals, making them the only real challenger to the notoriety and payouts of marlin and billfish tournaments. These events are televised, with millions of anglers tuning in to the biggest events, and viewership is only increasing. As such, the competition between the anglers is fierce, the pressure is always on, and any advantage is hungrily sought by the professional anglers whose entire livelihood and legacy can be predicated on just a single fish. That said, every day anglers tend to be the very best tinkerers and innovators, and with largemouth bass constituting upward of 43 percent of the total angling effort in the United States, it's no wonder so many lures and tackle have been created in a garage, basement, or at a work desk.

One of the hottest trends currently in the wide world of largemouth lures is fishing large swimbaits. Swimbait fishing for largemouth arose in the 1980s in California, where anglers initially wanted lures to catch 30- and 40-pound (14 to 18 kg) landlocked stripers. In angling for the stripers, fishermen started incidentally catching gigantic 15- to 18-pound (7 to 8 kg) largemouth. First attributed to the legendary angler Allan Cole, swimbaits rapidly rose to prominence through the 1990s, and by the early 2000s their popularity exploded worldwide. Today, the variety of swimbait forms is immense, but most mimic a large baitfish in the 8- to 14-inch range (20 to 36 cm)—that's right, a bass lure that's over a foot long! Swimbaits can be wood, plastic, or rubber, and some are so realistic, it's hard even for the angler to tell they're not real—and this is why they're so productive. As the bass get old, they have seen thousands of lures and may have been caught hundreds of times. They become extremely wary and stop responding to traditional lures. The swimbait breaks through this because it's so realistic and so huge— it's too easy a meal to pass up. While many factory-produced swimbaits are relatively affordable, custom-built swimbaits can fetch incredible prices—the most in demand, hand-carved lures fetch hundreds of dollars, and even a few select lures exceed a thousand. That may just be the best, most dramatic representation of the devotion anglers feel for the beloved largemouth.

# MUSKELLUNGE

| | |
|---|---|
| **DIFFICULTY** | **· 50 INCHES (1.3 M) ·**<br>**TROPHY SIZE** |

| | |
|---|---|
| **PERFECT SPOT** | St. Lawrence River, Ontario, Canada;<br>Green Bay of Lake Michigan, USA |
| **PREFERRED HABITAT** | Musky live in cool and cold waters, including both deep rivers and lakes, with an optimum temperature of 50 to 70°F (10 to 21°C). They need ample forage, primarily bait fish, and they prefer lying in heavy cover and ambushing prey that gets too close. They hang around stumps or rocky bars deep in vegetative cover. |
| **SEASON** | The best time to catch a trophy is early or late in the season, which varies by region. In summer months, fishing early in the day is your best bet, and in deeper water. Ice fishing for musky can also be productive. |
| **TOP TECHNIQUE** | Large live baits (such as suckers) are the best, but many anglers like trolling or throwing giant lures (over 10 inches, or 25 cm) such as glide baits, spinners, bucktails, and jerk baits. |
| **AVERAGE SIZE** | 25 to 35 inches (64 to 91 cm) |
| **RECORD SIZE LOCATION & DATE** | 67 pounds 8 ounces (31 kg), 60 ½ inches (1.6 m); Wisconsin, 1949 |

LAKES AND PONDS

## WHEN IT COMES TO FRESHWATER FISH, THE MUSKELLUNGE IS

one of the most hallowed. The love and devotion to "musky" is cultlike, and fishermen and -women who pursue these giant, toothy creatures are in a club that includes the most obsessed billfish anglers and diehard trout "bums." That is, for those that cite musky as their passion, there is typically no other species that matters. The musky obsessed are truly and deeply fanatical—but in a wonderful, venerable way.

The reasons for this deep allegiance are many. The musky is a titan that stands (or rather swims) upon the very tippy top of the apex predator pyramid. Missile shaped, long and tubular, their pointed heads contain a gigantic mouth absolutely packed with long, razor sharp, canine-like teeth. Once a musky grabs hold with that massive maw, nothing escapes its grasp. They are a visually striking fish overall, with a dark eye and large gill plates, and a coloration that ranges from light green or silver to dark brown or bronze, with darker vertical bars or spots. They are a cool-water or cold-water species, and they feed most aggressively when the water is between 58 and 68°F (14 and 20°C). While similar to pike, they are much bigger on average, have a different coloration, and are limited to North America, while the pike is found throughout the world.

The musky is an incredible mix of aggression and subtlety. It has a gargantuan appetite and will attack and try to eat anything that moves in or on the water—from 5-pound (2.3 kg) bass or catfish to small waterfowl and even muskrats. There have even been attacks on swimmers' hands and feet, where the musky likely confused them for fleeing fish. Despite this appetite for massive prey, musky are also highly calculated, fussy, and, at times, even skittish. They also can be exceedingly difficult to coax out of their hiding places in underwater vegetation or woody structure, and even when an angler succeeds, they are notorious for following a lure and not striking. After 8 hours of casting for no strikes, watching a giant fish cruise behind your lure for almost the entire retrieve, only to turn off at the last second, is one of the biggest heartbreaks in the angling world. However, it's just a part of pursuing these elusive beasts. For this reason, they are famously known as the "fish of 10,000 casts," and landing even one musky in an outing is a resounding success. But when that one fish is landed, it brings with it a profound feeling of accomplishment that makes pursuing musky oh-so-addicting.

Lots of anglers fish for musky with large live baits—suckers and chubs are by far the most popular. However, most musky maniacs use gigantic, absurd lures. Most are between 8 and 12 inches (20 cm to 30 cm), but many exceed 15 or even 20 inches (38 cm or 51 cm), and there are plenty even larger than that, some weighing over 2 pounds (0.9 kg)! When you're targeting fish that are more than 50 inches (1.3 m) and 50 pounds (23 kg) with 700 teeth, there is almost no lure too big. Many are outlandish and bizarre, appearing as if out of a science fiction film, with massive curly tails, bulging eyes, and monstrous spinning metal blades.

One very specific technique often required for catching both musky and pike is what is referred to as the "figure eight." When a musky is just tailing a lure all the way to the boat, anglers will dip their rods entirely in the water at the last moment, about halfway down the length, and swing the rod in a figure eight motion with the lure 2 to 4 feet (0.6 to 1.2 m) outside the tip. Why the figure eight works is debated, but it likely has something to do with triggering the musky to "think" the bait is now vulnerable by turning broadside. Sometimes a figure eight will result in a strike even when the angler didn't realize a fish was there, either due to stained water or the fact the fish was down deep. It's something highly unique to musky fishing; most anglers consider it a required action and do it every cast, no matter what.

# NORTHERN PIKE

| | |
|---|---|
| <br>**DIFFICULTY** | **· 20 POUNDS (9 KG);<br>40 INCHES (1 M) ·**<br>**TROPHY SIZE** |

| | |
|---|---|
| **PERFECT SPOT** | Yukon River, United States; Loch Ness, Scotland |
| **PREFERRED HABITAT** | Pike inhabit rivers and lakes that have thermal refuges and stay under 70°F (21°C), even in summer, throughout the northern latitudes worldwide. They are adaptable but prefer heavy vegetation and woody structure out of any current. |
| **SEASON** | Pike can be caught year-round but are most aggressive early and late in the year. Pike make excellent ice fishing targets |
| **TOP TECHNIQUE** | There is no best, or wrong, way to catch pike. Most anglers cast lures such as spoons, spinners, and crankbaits, but using large live baits or trolling is also popular. Fly fishing with huge streamers can be exciting too. |
| **AVERAGE SIZE** | 5 to 15 pounds (2.3 to 7 kg);<br>25 to 35 inches (64 to 89 cm) |
| **RECORD SIZE LOCATION & DATE** | 55 pounds 1 ounce (25 kg);<br>Lake of Grefeern, Germany, 1986 |

# NORTHERN PIKE ARE AN ICONIC FISH WORLDWIDE. LONG AND

tubular, they look very similar to musky, and it can be extremely hard to tell them apart in the places the two fish overlap. Pike—also called northerns— have similarly large duck-bill mouths leading into a sloped head with an angry looking eye, and they have same fearsome, razor-sharp teeth. They have similar proportions, with long, tubular bodies that provide them with their lightning-fast attacks from a dead-still ambush. Pike tend to be light to dark green, with a stronger patterning of cream-colored spots when compared to the musky; though they can range from near silver to almost brown. They get big—more than 40 inches (1 m)—but they don't quite match the musky's even more massive bulk.

Pike are brash predators and are explosive with power and impact driven by their streamlined and highly muscled bodies. During the peak of the season, it's hard to come up with a lure or bait the pike won't hit. Fishing the shallows during the cooler times of the year is often the most exciting, with heart-stopping moments as a pike annihilate lures at top speed, often within sight of the angler. Many anglers will utilize subsurface presentations for pike, but they'll routinely blast topwater lures too, ruthlessly launching themselves out of the water in pursuit. That said, like musky, for large chunks of the season pike are notorious for staying down deep and trailing behind trolled or retrieved baits for long distances, only to turn off for no reason at all. At these times, they need to be convinced to hit by aggressively twitching or sweeping the rod, and a figure eight at the boat side is a key trick to persuading these finicky fish to commit at the last moment.

Pike have a wide geographic distribution throughout the Northern Hemisphere of the world. Their populations stretch from coast to coast in North America, through most of Northern Europe, and across Russia all the way to the Pacific coast. They are a sneaky fish and love to tuck into heavy aquatic vegetation where their camouflage allows them to strike unwary prey that swim by. Being in more northern latitudes with lower human populations, pike waters are often pristine with little development. The remote lakes of Alaska, Russia, or Norway are some of the wildest in the world, requiring a float plane to reach, and anglers often spot everything from bald eagles and grizzlies to caribou and wolves while fishing. Yet, there is also excellent pike fishing in some highly populated places like some rivers outside Boston, Massachusetts, lakes within the city limits of Anchorage, Alaska, or the canals of Birmingham, England. Anglers of the north will also find pike fishing remains strong once the water has iced over, making them a year-round target.

One of the all-time most productive fishing lures, the "spoon" was created and earned its chops with pike fishing. The red and white Daredevle spoon was the innovative original, created by Lou Eppinger in 1906. This iconic classic is likely responsible for catching more pike than any other lure and is still catching tons of pike to this day. But beyond pike, other iterations of spoons in countless colors and shapes have caught just about every other species of fish in both freshwater and saltwater, and have become a pillar of the whole fishing community.

Like their brethren the musky, for the most devoted pike anglers there is no other fish that really matters. For pike fanatics, it's either fish for pike, or simply don't fish at all. The pike is an amazing balance between being big and fussy, but it is also aggressive and common enough to prevent fishing from being a perpetual grind (as it can be with musky). You must be focused and paying attention to catch pike, but if you are, you're likely to be rewarded with satisfying action on many of your outings. That's what makes them so resoundingly fun to pursue.

**LAKES AND PONDS**

**45**

# NORTHERN SNAKEHEAD

|  | · OVER 10 POUNDS (4.5 KG); 30 INCHES (76 CM) · |
|---|---|
| **DIFFICULTY** | **TROPHY SIZE** |

| | |
|---|---|
| **PERFECT SPOT** | Blackwater National Wildlife Refuge, United States; Lower Potomac River, United States |
| **PREFERRED HABITAT** | Snakehead live in any calm, shallow, and warm freshwater of 60 to 80°F (16 to 27°C) but prefer silty, muddy, and weedy waters. |
| **SEASON** | In North America, snakehead bite best from spring through fall. |
| **TOP TECHNIQUE** | Snakehead can be caught on everything from spinnerbaits to live minnows, but "frogging" (using a rubber frog in heavy weeds) is one of the most fun ways to catch them. |
| **AVERAGE SIZE** | 2 to 6 pounds (0.9 to 2.7 kg); 15 to 25 inches (38 to 64 cm) |
| **RECORD SIZE LOCATION & DATE** | 21 pounds (10 kg); Maryland, United States, 2023 |

# NORTHERN SNAKEHEAD ARE RUGGED, MENACING,

ill-tempered fish. They are long and tubular, and vaguely reminiscent of a thicker, stocky eel. Snakehead have a patterning similar to a python snake, and this, in combination with their flattened, broad heads, has given them their name. Snakehead have huge mouths filled with large, canine-like teeth. They are voracious, powerful, and opportunistic ambush attackers, and if they grab hold, nothing escapes their massive mouth and gnarly teeth.

Snakehead are survivors, able to adapt to the toughest water conditions. They can breathe air, which allows them to endure extremely oxygen-poor waters that are far from pristine, such as swamps, ditches, and canals. Young snakehead have been documented to live for multiple days out of water, and adults are even able to move short distances across land—an adaptation that helps them escape waterways that are likely to dry up. Snakehead can also survive in a huge spectrum of temperatures; in water as low as 32° F (0° C), they enter a suspended metabolic state called torpor. This is like hibernation and allows them to tolerate extended durations in near-freezing temperatures. Yet, they can also thrive in very poorly oxygenated waters at temperatures approaching 90°F (32°C).

Another interesting tidbit about snakehead is their defensive parenting. Once fry hatch, they ball up together in a large school, and the adults protect them from predators with wicked savagery. Anything that comes too close is assaulted and either killed, frightened away, or distracted and led away by the adults. While prespawn is the best time to target these fish, they will attack lures they perceive as a threat after they give birth. It's a different tactic, getting protective parents to bite your lure. It's more about making a racket, and making them angry, rather than presenting something they'd actually like to eat.

There's no guilt about disrupting their spawn either. The ugly truth is snakehead are an invasive species that made their way into the United States from Eastern Asia. They were first documented in California many decades ago; then a few were found in Maryland in 2002 and they have since spread throughout the East Coast and south to Florida. How they got to the States is a mystery, though it's likely they were imported with the illegal fish trade and then released. When they were discovered, their nasty attitude and appearance set off a firestorm in the media, where they acquired the name frankenfish, because of their ability to live anywhere and eat anything. Their precise impact on the native flora is still being studied, and while there are plans to try to remove or eradicate them from North America, for the time being they are beyond the point of containment. An angler should never introduce them to new waterways—beyond it being simply illegal, their voracious nature means they can quickly overwhelm the local flora (both bait and gamefish) and disrupt the native food web.

Those anglers who love snakehead the most agree that catching them on topwater lures is the most exciting method. They love how snakehead are brash, and will give chase to anything moving on the surface, and they will detonate on a popper, frog, or wake bait with explosive gusto. But what also makes them so fun is their notorious reputation for being wary, attentive, and spooky. They will not commit to a lure if they are aware of the angler nearby (either in a boat or kayak, or on the bank). Therefore, a good measure of stealth and finesse is necessary when hunting them, particularly in cleaner, shallow waters. Long casts and slow retrieves are advisable, and this builds a lot of suspense and anticipation. Then, when they take the lure and are hooked, dragging a 10-pound (5 kg) snakehead out of heavy cover can lead to some epic battles. It's a subtle game of cat and mouse, with an explosive finale.

# SMALLMOUTH BASS

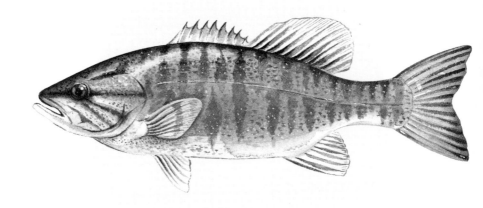

| | |
|---|---|
|  | **· 6 POUNDS (2.7 KG);**<br>**22 INCHES (56 CM) ·** |
| **DIFFICULTY** | **TROPHY SIZE** |

| | |
|---|---|
| **PERFECT SPOT** | Great Pond, Maine, United States;<br>Lake St. Clair, Ontario, Canada |
| **PREFERRED HABITAT** | Smallmouth are adaptable, but they love crayfish and are often found in places where that food source lives—humps, shoals, deeper water drop-offs, and in and around rocky and woody structures with an optimum water temperature from 60 to 75°F (15 to 24°C). |
| **SEASON** | Smallmouth can be caught year-round, including through the ice, but they feed most aggressively in the spring, early summer, and fall. |
| **TOP TECHNIQUE** | Jigs bumped along the bottom work like magic and the introduction of the Ned rig in recent years is a perfect, deadly technique. However, jig-like flies are very effective as well, including the legendary clouser minnow. |
| **AVERAGE SIZE** | ½ to 4 pounds (0.2 to 1.8 kg);<br>6 to 18 inches (15 to 45 cm) |
| **RECORD SIZE LOCATION & DATE** | 11 pounds 15 ounces (5 kg), 27 inches (66 cm);<br>Tennessee, United States, 1955 |

## THE SMALLMOUTH BASS IS THE SMALLER, BRASHER SIBLING

of the largemouth. They have a similar body shape to largemouth and—although their name suggests otherwise—a relatively large round mouth that is only slightly smaller than a largemouth's. They vary widely in coloration, from pale and almost green to bronze or very dark brown; in many waters, they have the nickname "bronze back" for this reason. Smallmouth also have large tails, though they may not quite match up in that department to the largemouth. Overall, an unremarkable-looking fish, but one that makes up for it in their temperament and attitude.

Smallmouth are native to the Great Lakes, Southern Canada, and Upper Mississippi River basin, but have been introduced to nearly every state in the United States, including Hawaii, and every other continent (excluding Antarctica). They coexist in many of the same waters as largemouth, but "smallies" prefer cooler water; they are most comfortable in mid-60 to mid-70° water (18 to 24°C), roughly a 10-degree (6°C) difference from largemouth (who prefer temperatures over 70° (21°C)). You will find them thriving in lakes and ponds alongside largemouth and walleye, but they also excel in moving water, where they may coexist alongside brown and rainbow trout. They will hunker down into vegetation like the largemouth, but you're more likely to find them on rocky shoals, in woody structures, and along drop-offs.

Smallies will eat anything they can fit in their mouths, and they viciously attack anything that moves—from bugs and minnows to sunfish, frogs, and mice. As a result, you can use just about anything to catch them, from poppers and spinners to minnows and worms. However, there is no question what the favorite forage of a smallie is: crayfish. By some accounts, in many waterways crayfish (also known as crawfish) make upward of 70 percent of smallies' total diet. While largemouth will never pass up a crayfish, more trophy smallmouth have likely been caught with crayfish-mimicking lures and flies than anything else. If you're trying to tempt fussy smallies, or fool a trophy, the way to often bypass their crafty little brains is by tossing a crayfish imitator at them. They have a compulsion to strike at a crayfish, and this makes jigs, Ned rigs, and crayfish-imitating crank baits super popular for smallies. They're also a world-renowned and deeply loved fly-rod fish across the world. The clouser minnow is a fly that was created in 1987 by Bob Clouser for fooling smallies, and it has since become one of the most versatile and important flies of all time. It has caught a dizzying number of local and international records and has hooked everything from brook trout and steelhead to bonefish and sailfish. The clouser is a pivotal fly in fishing history, chalked up to the smallie.

While the differences between smallies and largemouth include size and preferred ecological niche (where they live and hunt), it's really their attitude that sets smallies apart. To put it bluntly, smallies are ferocious. This difference also gets to the heart of the most asked question for the smallmouth-uninitiated: Why would a fisherman choose to pursue the smaller smallmouth if they live in the same waters as the larger largemouth? For the smallmouth aficionado, the reasons are many, but at the top of the list is the smallies' belligerent attitude and all-out, utterly explosive, unyielding fight. Pound for pound, there are few fish that fight harder than a smallie—freshwater or saltwater. Compared to the "diesel" largemouth, smallies are "jet fueled." And while they will run fast and hard, more than anything they are known for heroic leaps. Like a rodeo bull when the gate is pulled, smallies go immediately to full speed and launch themselves skyward at the merest prickle of a hook point. Certainly, there are many species that are great "jumpers," but smallies must be counted among the very best. Frankly, in waters they share with either typically sized trout or largemouth, there is no question who the ultimate fighter is: the smallie reigns supreme. They pull hard, run hard, dive hard, jump hard, and make it hard to not fall in love with these mighty fish.

# WALLEYE

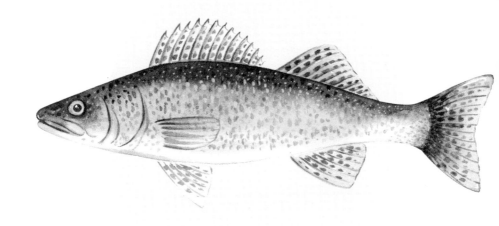

| <br>**DIFFICULTY** | **· 25 TO 30 INCHES (64 TO 76 CM); REGION SPECIFIC ·**<br>**TROPHY SIZE** |
| --- | --- |

| | |
| --- | --- |
| **PERFECT SPOT** | Lake of the Woods, United States; Bay of Quinte, Canada |
| **PREFERRED HABITAT** | Lakes and slow-moving rivers with thermal refuges—under 70°F (21°C) even in summer—preferably with shallow, soft-bottom areas for spawning. Walleye can be found around points and reefs, but also move around a lot during low-light hours and at night. |
| **SEASON** | Walleye can be caught year-round, including through the ice. |
| **TOP TECHNIQUE** | During the day, jigging lures or bait vertically over woody or rocky structure is the most popular walleye method. Moving around shallower areas and fan casting at night is your best bet at consistent trophy success. |
| **AVERAGE SIZE** | 10 to 20 inches (25 to 51 cm) |
| **RECORD SIZE LOCATION & DATE** | 25 pounds 4 ounces (11 kg), 41 inches (1 m); Tennessee, United States, 1960 |

# WALLEYE SEEM UNEXCEPTIONAL AT FIRST GLANCE. THEY

typically are uniform off-green or bronze in color, with slight speckling on their flanks and subtle patterning of darker spots. They are a common body shape for a freshwater fish: tubular, with a narrow, pointed head, and average-sized tail. They are found in slow or still water, and they hide in woody and rocky structures, particularly around points and reefs. They leave these places at night and during low-light hours to stalk prey, invading the shallows hunting bait fish, crustaceans, and invertebrates. All of these characteristics are typical for many fish, and not particularly exciting.

But look a little closer, and you will find that the walleye is a specialized and exceptional predator. Chief among their unique traits is an abnormally large eye. This underlies their incredible ability to see in low light and in murky, cloudy, and stirred-up water. They can't see detail well (most fish cannot), but walleye have some of the largest rod receptors in their eyes of the entire animal kingdom. Rod receptors are what collect light, and as a result, compared to bait fish (and just about every other animal), the walleye has virtual night vision: nothing sees like a walleye. They use this sight to feed with ruthless efficiency. Walleye do not chase or wait in ambush. Instead, they cruise the shallows in the depths of the night or around the margins of the day, snatching up prey that simply can't see them coming. This behavior raises an important point: if you really want to catch a giant, you should forgo sleep and head out into the night on a blustery autumn evening—this is the hour and season of the walleye.

Walleye are not known to be hard fighting, but instead have become an obsession for anglers for two main reasons: their accessibility and their fickle nature. In Canada and the Northern United States, most cool-water fishing holes have walleye. As long as the deeper portions of a lake or river stay under 70°F (20°C) through the summer, and there's plenty of baitfish they can eat, walleye will thrive. This means many anglers are drawn into the immense world of fishing by walleye: they are readily available to catch "right around the corner" for so many anglers.

For the hard-core walleye addict, accessibility is not the reason they dream of walleye night and day. Instead, there's something a bit exotic and implicitly challenging about walleye that drives anglers nuts. During daylight, they are down deep, turned off, and stay jammed in tight to woody or rocky structures— it's often very difficult to draw them out. Fickle and wary, they require precision, finesse, and patience. Jigging for these fish can be maddening, but exciting when it produces results. Then during dawn, dusk, and at night (and sometimes during windy weather), everything is flipped upside-down. They move around constantly, covering many miles across expansive areas. In fact, walleye can cover vast distances— miles each and every night, and over 200 miles (322 km) during spawning season. For this reason, they are hard to pattern. The angler must be aggressive in response and use lures that also cover ground (like crankbaits, soft plastics, and spinners) and be constantly on the move. The challenge of finding big walleye and enticing them to strike can be frustrating for even the most skilled angler, but this means that when a massive walleye does strike, it's rewarding and intoxicating.

Finally, walleye are a year-round fish, and there is a subculture of hardened anglers that only target them through the ice. These men and women venture out to fish in some of the coldest, most bitter weather imaginable, during the shortest days and longest nights of the year. Walleye can feed aggressively in winter, and ice anglers find there is something particularly rewarding about pursuing the fish through a tiny window they create themselves. It's such a different feeling than floating on the surface in a boat, or standing on the bank casting, and it's another flavor of what makes the walleye special.

# ALLIGATOR GAR

| | |
|---|---|
| **DIFFICULTY** | **· OVER 150 POUNDS (68 KG); 7 FEET (2.1 M) ·**<br>**TROPHY SIZE** |

| | |
|---|---|
| **PERFECT SPOT** | Trinity River, Texas, United States; St. Catherine Creek National Wildlife Refuge, Mississippi, United States |
| **PREFERRED HABITAT** | Slow moving rivers in South Central United States. The largest gar are typically found in larger bodies of water, but smaller alligator gar can be found in small tributaries with an optimum water temperature greater than 70°F (21°C). These fish associate with places to hide and ambush prey, like woody structure or corner eddies. |
| **SEASON** | Alligator gar bite best during the warmest months of the year. |
| **TOP TECHNIQUE** | Chunks of freshly caught fish are best, rigged with a very sharp hook. |
| **AVERAGE SIZE** | 10 to 100 pounds (5 to 45 kg); 3 to 6 feet (0.9 to 1.8 m) |
| **RECORD SIZE LOCATION & DATE** | 283 pounds (128 kg); Texas, United States, 2023 |

## ALLIGATOR GAR ARE APTLY NAMED—THEY ARE HUGE, TOOTHY,

intimidating looking fish that could easily be mistaken for actual alligators in the muddy, slow-moving waters of their native rivers. They are the second largest freshwater fish in North America and can reach at least 300 pounds (136 kg) and over 8 feet long (2 m). They have elongated, torpedo-shaped bodies covered in huge scales that act like armor. Yet, their hallmark is still their gator-like mouths, which are packed with rows of three different kinds of overlapping teeth, adding up to over 1,000 teeth total—all very pointy and sharp. It's a gruesome looking set of chompers designed to grab unsuspecting prey, and never, ever let go.

Despite its fearsome appearance and gigantic size, the alligator gar is a wary and sly fish. For centuries they were reviled, being blamed for attacking swimmers, and decimating other fish stocks (such as bass and catfish). Both these are falsehoods, and even when they reach a couple hundred pounds, they are very skittish, sensitive to boat traffic, and flee at the first sign of danger (even on the bank). This means finding and fooling a gar requires an immense amount of patience and finesse. Their populations are small, so locating them requires moving around and off the beaten path adventuring, and then tossing out bait and waiting. The waters they live in are muddy and visibility is next to nothing; an angler must simply do their research, find a likely spot, and then fish it blind.

Gar are notorious for picking up a bait and then simply swimming around with it in the toothy part of their mouths, which are impenetrable to a hook. This might last for 10 seconds, or it might be a minute. As a result, an angler must let the fish attempt to swallow the bait, and this takes patience—upward of a minute before setting the hook. Then, when, or if, an angler does get a good hookset, they're in for a battle they will often lose. Large gar are very strong, and they will run hard, diving for the bottom, and even run into deadfalls, stumps, or anything else they can use to break the line. Gar live a long time—upward of 100 years. Local anglers believe they learn from prior experiences as to how to get off the line. Gar also can breathe air and are good at thriving in waters with very little oxygen, so they are highly resistant to fatigue and built for long battles. The fight with an alligator gar is always intense and wracked with anxiety.

While it's possible to catch alligator gar on lures (and even flies), the vast majority are caught on chunks of bait. The most diehard gar hunters will catch native fish like buffalo or carp and cut it into chunks. From there, two different rigging methods are used. The first is a large treble hook skewered into the flesh of the bait, often with a slip float to keep it off the bottom. More recently anglers have switched to using a smaller, super strong single bait hook. They will attach it to the bait with rigging floss or zip ties, so that the hook is not in the bait. These relatively smaller hooks (often size 3/0 or 4/0) with their thinner wire can pierce the hard parts of the mouth before the gar tries to swallow the bait. This means the angler doesn't have to wait as long to set the hook, decreasing the chance the gar will drop the bait, and these small hooks do a lot less damage to released fish. With gar populations dramatically decreased due to habitat destruction and overharvest, releasing fish healthy has become a priority.

The gar is a hard fish to catch, and the landing ratio is very low. Yet, gar anglers are extremely dedicated to catching this monstrous fish. When a fish requires this much work to find, hook, and land, it makes each landed individual a trophy of extreme value.

# BROOK TROUT

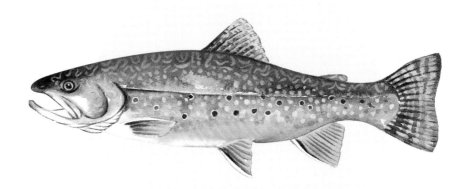

| | |
|---|---|
| **DIFFICULTY** | **· 12 TO 25 INCHES (30 TO 64 CM);**<br>**REGION SPECIFIC ·**<br>**TROPHY SIZE** |

| | |
|---|---|
| **PERFECT SPOT** | Class A Wild Streams; Central Pennsylvania, United States; Eastern Labrador, Canada |
| **PREFERRED HABITAT** | Brookies are the trout of headwater streams and creeks, but they are also found in spring-fed ponds and bogs, cold-water lakes, and tidal streams and rivers along their northern range. They enjoy a water temperature of 45 to 65°F (7 to 18°C). |
| **SEASON** | Brookies are sensitive to water temperature, and the best fishing is in the spring and fall. |
| **TOP TECHNIQUE** | A very light fly rod and dry flies on small streams is the best. Nymphs and streamers are favorites on larger rivers. |
| **AVERAGE SIZE** | 3 to 8 inches (8 to 20 cm), region specific |
| **RECORD SIZE LOCATION & DATE** | 14 pounds 8 ounces (7 kg), 31½ inches (80 cm); Ontario, Canada, 1915 |

## WITHOUT QUESTION, BROOK TROUT ARE ONE OF THE MOST

beautiful fish in the world. They aren't bright or fluorescent, but instead they are striking in contrast. They have a subtle crisscross pattern across their jet-black backs, their sides transition to a deep burnt orange and then sunflower yellow, eventually ending in a cream-colored belly. Their fins range from pale yellow to dark orange, with a stripe of bright white along the edge. Running along their sides is a kaleidoscope of spots of red or orange, yellow, and blue, like a dusting of stars.

Beautiful, yes, but it is the ferocity of a brook trout that often first draws anglers to the fish, and then ultimately hooks them for life. They are one of the smallest trout species, but they are arguably the mightiest. "Brookies" attack their prey with a zeal that is legendary. A hooked brookie will put a deep bend in a light fly rod, and they run, jump, cartwheel, and fight the angler every inch of the way. During the landing, trying to net or hold a brookie is often a feat in itself. The power unleashed by these small fish is truly incredible.

While the fight may be heroic, the actual fishing is all about being subtle and stealthy. Brookies spook easily, so throwing a shadow on the water is certain to send them rocketing out of a run and up under a cutbank or into a deep pool. A splash while wading, heavy footfalls on the bank, or even a poorly placed cast can turn them off from feeding entirely. For this reason, fishing for brookies must be done slowly, and intentionally, with considerable stalking of the fish and planning of the approach. It often feels more like hunting than fishing, but the adrenaline and intensity of sneaking up on a fish, seeing it take a fly, and then the savagery of the fight—all in the tiniest of waterways—is what ignites passion in the angler's heart

The other aspect of the brookie that draws anglers and can forge them into lifelong sportsmen is the majestic and wild places brookies live. Since they prefer pristine headwaters, they are often found in the wildest places along their native range. Wild brookies have persisted through the last ice age and eke out a living in the mountain creeks and remote spring-fed ponds. Adventurous anglers trek into these wild places, seeking unnamed ribbons of water found on a topographical map, or glimpsed on a satellite image. There is no guide to these places, and no online tutorial; it is up to the angler to discover if the fish are there, or not. If you do the same, you may be surprised where small, isolated populations of brookies still thrive.

Brookies are highly adaptable and will go to great lengths to survive in their home waters. They have been known to go underground into springs to survive hot summers and climb streams with slopes over 20 percent to get to headwater flows. Despite their tenacity, in most areas of the United States, brookies are small, maxing out at 8 to 10 inches (20 to 25 cm), but along their northern ranges—Maine, Quebec, New Brunswick, and onward north to the Hudson Bay—brookies can grow preposterously large. Giants in Canada can reach 20 to 25 inches (51 to 63 cm).

To catch brook trout, you can use the simplest tackle: a hook, some line, and a worm. However, for most anglers that consider brookies their passion, the fly rod is the preferred method, and fishing is primarily a spring and fall undertaking. Fly selection typically comes down to matching the locally available forage and will yield you the most fish, especially the largest, most experienced fish. Don't be fooled by their diminutive size: brookies are apex predators, no matter if they're 3 or 23 inches (8 or 58 cm) long. If targeting fish over 8 inches (20 cm), even in tiny streams, you can (and should) cast larger brown or rainbow trout streamers to brookies—or even mouse flies.

# BROWN TROUT

| |  **· 20 TO 30 INCHES (51 TO 76 CM);** **MORPH DEPENDENT ·** |
|---|---|
| **DIFFICULTY** | **TROPHY SIZE** |

| | |
|---|---|
| **PERFECT SPOT** | Kahurangi National Park, New Zealand; Battenkill River, United States |
| **PREFERRED HABITAT** | Browns are river fish that need cool, clean, moving water with an optimum temperature of 45 to 65 °F (7 to 18°C). They inhabit all parts of a river based on the time of year and feed available. |
| **SEASON** | Spring and fall are best, but they can certainly be caught all year round. |
| **TOP TECHNIQUE** | Fly fishing for brown trout is undeniably special, particularly with small dry flies. However, fishing for large fish with spoons and swimmers can be very rewarding. Mousing at night for browns is especially intense and can lead to trophies. |
| **AVERAGE SIZE** | 8 to 15 inches (20 to 38 cm); location dependent |
| **RECORD SIZE LOCATION & DATE** | 44 pounds 5 ounces (20 kg), 38 ½ inches (98 cm); Oahu Canal, New Zealand, 2020 |

# THROUGHOUT HISTORY, BROWN TROUT HAVE INSPIRED

countless anglers, drawing them into the world of angling and changing their lives, forever. There is a mountain of books, articles, and poetry written about fishing for brown trout, probably more than any other species. The very first documented writings of fly fishing are attributed to Claudius Aelianus in his book *On the Nature of Animals*, which was published around 200 CE. In it, Aelianus describes how flies made of feathers and fur were used to catch a "fish with speckled skins" in Macedonia, which many historians presume was likely a brown trout. Therefore, at minimum, anglers have been writing about the pursuit of brown trout with flies for over 1,800 years.

Brown trout are native to most of Europe and Western Asia, but have been introduced to every continent, except Antarctica, and almost every state in the United States. They can survive in all the same places brook trout and rainbow trout can, yet are a bit more hardy and able to handle higher water temperatures. Browns have a typical trout body: tubular, with average proportions and a broad tail. They get their name from their tawny or off-brown coloration along their dorsal, which transitions to yellow or golden sides. They are also typically speckled with orange, red, dark brown, or black spots, which vary in pattern based on where they are found in the world.

Compared to other sport fish, there is a wide spectrum to the way brown trout look and behave across the world. Part of this has to do with the three commonly recognized "morphs" or "ecotypes" of the browns: river, lake, and sea-run. Each is so named by where they are most likely to be found and reflects the adaptability of browns. Few other fish can live in as diverse environments as the browns—anywhere from headwater streams to mountain lakes, to the open oceans and so many others in between. Overall size, patterning and coloration, aggressiveness, lifespan, spawning time, and many other factors are influenced by the type of water you find a brown living in. Sea-run trout and large-lake browns in particular are quite a bit different than the "typical" river or stream brown trout that most anglers target. They are much broader and heavily shouldered, with thick, hooked jaws, and they get massive. These fish regularly exceed 30 pounds (14 kg), with speculation that a 50-pound fish is out there somewhere right now, just waiting to exceed the current world record.

And yet, complicating things even further, there are distinct populations within these morphs (river, lake, and sea-run) that have been separated for millennia. These "strains" can be so different from each other that they look like different species. Just because browns are found in similar looking rivers in Europe and North America, doesn't mean they'll look or act anything like one another. The diversity is remarkable, and these strains are named after the waterways in which they are found—for example, the famous Loch Leven strain, or the von Behr strain. In North America, the initial population started out with just a couple of strains, but with many new strains introduced and natural evolution, it's a total mash-up. Regardless, all these morphs, subpopulations, and environmental separations have made brown trout one of the most genetically diverse species on Earth. According to some findings, there is greater genetic diversity between brown trout in just a few regions of Europe, than there is between any group of human beings on Earth.

These fish are beautiful, rugged, and malleable, but that is not what calls to anglers. Instead, it is their attitude and athleticism. Brown trout are intensely frustrating, a top contender for the most fussy, finicky fish. Even in rivers with few anglers, they can require a high degree of precision in fly or lure selection, as well as accurate casting and spot-on presentation. But on waters that are heavily pressured—where they see lots of flies and lures—old, wild, and experienced browns can feel impossible to catch. They are notorious for snubbing the most realistic flies, even when they're feeding heavily on something that appears identical to our human eyes. Their awareness of the surrounding waters and banks is also astounding, and the slightest mistake by the angler can send them bolting for cover. As they grow older, they also feed more under the cover of foul weather and in complete darkness. This means catching one during daylight on a fly can be challenging and complicated, requiring a whole host of specialized skills developed and honed through many hours on the water. It's no wonder many anglers treat every cast like it's the only shot they'll get at the fish all day.

Once hooked, the most difficult part is over, but there is still a significant hurdle to get over: brown trout fight like raging bulls. They go ballistic, and will run hard, zigzagging through the river, or diving for deep water, and also jumping repeatedly. It can be chaotic, and since anglers are typically forced to use very light line to fool the fish, they are now faced with having to land that fish on that very same line. It can be nerve wracking, and many a brown trout angler will scream in exaltation when that big fish finally slides into the landing net. Accomplishing that feat is a feeling of pure bliss. Even if you've done it 1,000 times, it never gets old.

While they're fussy and crafty, many anglers don't realize just how aggressive brown trout can be. The image of a trout gently rising to sip a tiny fly off the surface is only one dimension of the brown. They are top-level

predators, and when they get big, they will eat anything and can attack with the ferocity of any of the other great sportfish. One way anglers capitalize on this is by "mousing" for browns. As the name implies, fly anglers use flies that look like mice, which they fish after dark, dragging across the surface of pools and quieter areas of

rivers. In some places worldwide, including the United
States, New Zealand, and Argentina, this is one of the
best ways to catch a trophy-sized brown. It doesn't have
the elegance, grace, or poetry of dry fly fishing, but trades
that for a visceral, violent experience where the angler
must fish by sound and feel, rather than sight.

Despite their cunning, wariness, and brute strength,
browns are caught with a wide spectrum of methods—
bait, lures, and flies. If the goal is catching a trophy-sized fish, then bait fish
patterned flies and lures are often the best choice, fished around low-light hours.
Don't be too intimidated, either; plenty are caught with minnow lures or spoons,
and you don't have to be a fly fisherman. That being said, there is something
triumphant about catching a big, hardened brown trout on a miniscule dry fly.
There's a real art to it, and the skill it takes to pick the right fly, fool a stubborn
fish with a perfect drift, and then fight it with little light takes time to develop.
The anglers who routinely take on this challenge are astoundingly focused,
hone their skills constantly (on and off the water), and study their quarry with
the fervent obsession of a lifelong scholar. It may look like obsession, or even
addiction, to those who don't fish, but they don't understand the feeling of
satisfaction that comes with landing a trophy brown.

# CATFISH

|  | · CHANNEL CATFISH: 15 POUNDS (7 KG); BLUE CATFISH: 80 POUNDS (36 KG); FLATHEAD CATFISH: 60 POUNDS (27 KG) · |
|---|---|
| **DIFFICULTY** | **TROPHY SIZE** |

| | |
|---|---|
| **PERFECT SPOT** | Kerr Lake, United States; Mississippi River, United States |
| **PREFERRED HABITAT** | Catfish can thrive in a variety of freshwater (some can handle brackish, too), but they are primarily (and evolutionarily) river fish that prefer moving water. They are most likely to be found in eddies and seams at edges of faster moving water; they have a very wide optimum water temperature of 50 to 85°F (10 to 29°C). |
| **SEASON** | Fishing for catfish is a year-round endeavor. However, spring, early summer, and fall are peak. |
| **TOP TECHNIQUE** | Chunks of cut bait is the most popular method, held to the bottom with sinkers. Trophy cats are often taken on live bait, and some catfish will readily chase lures. |
| **AVERAGE SIZE** | Channel catfish: 2 to 10 pounds (1 to 5 kg) <br> Blue and flathead catfish: 5 to 30 pounds (2.3 to 14 kg) |
| **RECORD SIZE LOCATION & DATE** | Channel catfish: 58 pounds (26 kg), 47 inches (1.2 m); South Carolina, United States, 1964 <br> Blue catfish: 143 pounds (65 kg), 57 inches (1.5 m); North Carolina, United States 2011 <br> Flathead catfish: 123 pounds (56 kg), 61 inches (1.6 m); Kansas, United States, 1998 |

# CATFISH ARE LIKELY TO WIN THE AWARD FOR "MOST

common": you can find them anywhere, from crystal clear, pristine rivers and small, muddy ponds, to the largest lakes and rivers in the world. They are also one of the most recognizable fish, characterized by their catlike whiskers (where they get their name), flat heads, and relatively small eyes situated high on the head. Despite their general abundance, for landlocked anglers, catfish are one of the largest fish they can tangle with. Catfish of various species are commonly found over 15 pounds (7 kg), and blue catfish and flatheads in particular are giants, and can easily exceed 100 pounds (45 kg). The wels catfish is the largest, with the world record currently standing at almost 10 feet (3 m) long, and documented catches over 300 pounds (136 kg). These are the exceptional giants, but even channel catfish—the most common "cats" in North America—can exceed 10 pounds (5 kg) easily.

Despite their size, many anglers have the preconceived notion that catfish are a lazy, muddy-watered, boring fish that unrefined fishermen target as a last resort. This notion is absolutely, utterly, and totally wrong. Catfish can be outright savage, predatory fish that put up phenomenal, protracted fights, and experienced cats can be some of the craftiest fish in the water. This then requires the most devoted cat-hunters to be equally crafty, devoted, and hard-core. They are observant, meticulous, and constantly thinking of new ways to catch larger fish. This is because, contrary to what many anglers think, catfish will not just eat anything at any time. Trophy-sized fish can get fussy and easily turned off by a whole host of factors, including boat noise, steel leaders, or even bug spray or sunscreen that gets on bait from an angler's hands. This is all due to the incredibly impressive array of senses a catfish possesses— many of which seem almost alien.

Like all fish, catfish have a lateral line that can detect subtle vibrations in the water, and an inner ear that discerns sound waves. They detect and identify creatures and objects in the water simply by the way they create vibration. Catfish don't need to see a crayfish or a sunfish to know exactly what and where it is: if it moves, and it's relatively close, they know precisely right down to the millimeter. Interestingly, a catfish's hearing, especially at higher frequencies, is much better than most game fish—much better than a bass or panfish. Plus, many catfish can actually see quite well (for a fish) and use their eyesight in clear water for hunting—including actively chasing down prey.

Catfish can also smell food from great distances, even in miniscule concentrations. Using 2 nostril-like holes at the front of their head that lead to special sensory cells, channel cats can track certain smells associated with baitfish (technically amino acids, which are the building blocks of proteins) at a concentration of 1 part per 100 million. That's roughly 12 drops of liquid in a full-size swimming pool. This means nothing escapes their scent detection, and catfish are constantly aware of what is available to eat over great distances, in all directions at once, through sound, sight, and smell. But perhaps even more remarkable is that catfish are also coated head-to-tail in taste buds. They can taste food by rubbing along it with their sides, and even from several feet away without touching it at all. In essence, catfish are bristling with an array of incredible senses that make them both formidable predators and amazing sportfish.

If you want to catch trophy-sized cats, whether that's an 80-pound (36 kg) blue or a 12-pound (5.4 kg) channel, it's not as simple as throwing out some dead bait in a random spot, and then taking a nap. Trophy catfish anglers study their waters intensely, focusing on specific bodies of water where giants are known to roam. They seek out the most likely holes, eddies, and current seams where catfish congregate. Once they have their spots nailed down, they fish these special areas only when they have the best chance at catching. This is based on additional factors they track closely, such as storm fronts, water temperature, current speed (and water volume), and even fishing pressure. Trophy anglers are also meticulous about where they cast their baits, how they move through the currents, and where they end up on the bottom. Just like any other fishery, the largest cats are taken by a small percentage of highly skilled, observant, and detail-oriented fishermen. There's an element of luck to any fishing, but if you want to catch large cats, you want to leave as little to chance as possible.

Catfish are also very strong, hard fighters. Particularly if they're hooked in current, catfish will take long runs and use their broad and heavy bodies to put serious strain on your tackle. They constantly hunt for the bottom, so trying to lift them to the surface can feel like trying to pull up a pile of bricks—a pile of bricks that pulls back. This goes for all sizes of catfish, but large cats can challenge anglers even fishing with extra-heavy tackle designed for large saltwater species. Sometimes, even a 50-pound (23 kg) test line and 100-pound (45 kg) leaders aren't enough when a big flat head or blue surges into a rockpile or under a bank. All catfish are resistant to fatigue and will not relent—most anglers agree that they pull even harder once they get close to the boat and sense real danger.

For certain, no matter how serious you are about them, catfish are easiest to catch with bait. If you're just starting out with catfish, and aren't trophy hunting, you can use just about anything—some anglers even swear by hot dogs or french fries! Most anglers will use some form of dead or cut bait, because it's easy to fish on the bottom in the currents where catfish are most likely to be found. That said, a very big "secret" about catching trophy cats is this: the largest fish prefer live bait. As they grow old (catfish can live upward of 30 years), they are more discerning and feed more methodically. They become wary, sly, and hard to coax out of heavy structure, or trigger to feed, and dead bait often won't cut it—it has to be swimming. Many top catfish anglers will further urge you to use live bait that you catch in the same water you're fishing in: panfish, large minnows, and other forage species are best.

Blues and channel cats in particular are known to chase baitfish just like a bass, or even rise to insects on the surface like a trout. As anglers continue to break down preconceived notions about catfish, more and more are being caught on lures retrieved on spinning tackle. That's right: catfish will chase down and attack even fast moving, aggressive lures. Given their eyesight and ability to sense even the most subtle vibration, it's no wonder they will—at times—happily hammer a crankbait or even a topwater popper. Catching 20- or 30-pound (9 or 18 kg) catfish on a lure is an exciting prospect many anglers don't even realize is possible and opens up a whole new world of possibilities. Enterprising anglers are now even regularly targeting catfish with fly fishing gear across the world, which comes with a whole host of additional challenges, including getting the fly down to where the fish is, and fooling all those formidable senses with nothing more than fur and feathers. Taking this to the ultimate extreme, giant Wels catfish have even begun to fall to fly anglers as well.

# CHINOOK SALMON

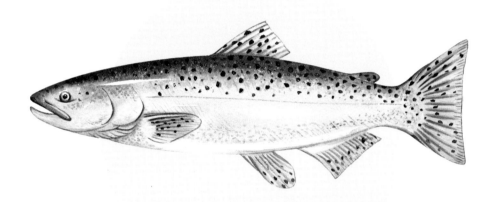

| | |
|---|---|
| **DIFFICULTY** | **TROPHY SIZE** |
| | · 60 POUNDS (27 KG) · |

| | |
|---|---|
| **PERFECT SPOT** | Waitaki River, New Zealand;<br>Kenai River, Alaska, United States |
| **PREFERRED HABITAT** | Chinook live most of their lives in the open ocean, but they return to large rivers to spawn. In these rivers, you will find them in deeper pools and along current seams with an optimum water temperature of 45 to 55°F (7 to 12°C). |
| **SEASON** | Large adults make two spawning runs—one in late summer and fall, the other in later fall into winter. They can be caught throughout this period.<br>Note: The native pacific chinook population is struggling due to overfishing. Before you head out, make sure to check state regulations. |
| **TOP TECHNIQUE** | Fly fishing for king salmon can feel like the pinnacle of the technique. However, floating baits and casting lures work well. In the ocean, trolling bait or lures is the way to go. |
| **AVERAGE SIZE** | 25 to 40 pounds (11 to 18 kg) |
| **RECORD SIZE LOCATION & DATE** | 97 pounds 4 ounces (44 kg);<br>Kenai River, Alaska, United States, 1985 |

# CHINOOK SALMON ARE ALSO KNOWN AS KING SALMON, AND

the reason for this nickname is obvious: they are the largest salmon species, with many fish in the 40- to 50-pound (18 to 23 kg) range caught each year by anglers, and some 100-pound-plus (45 kg) fish caught commercially. They are notoriously strong and beastly fighters, even when matched up pound for pound with coho or steelhead. When they take a fly or lure, they will explode downstream, ripping line off the reel, and even taking flight in dramatic jumps, cartwheels, and backflips. They're so big and so fast, there's nothing quite like them in the rivers in which they swim. They bring the power and energy of the ocean into the river.

Fresh from the sea, chinook are a plain, clean looking fish. They are undramatic in their overall silver coloration and typical stocky, trout-like body, which ends in a broad, wide tail. They are known for their characteristic black gums and mouth, but otherwise are unremarkable. However, when they return from the sea and travel upriver to spawn, their bodies start to break down. They will start to turn black, and then bronze-brown, and ultimately bright red at the very end of their lives. This makes them more dramatic looking but signals the end of their lives. Salmon do not return to the ocean once the spawn is complete; in a dramatic commitment to the next generation, the freshwater degrades their bodies, and they succumb to the strain of their epic journey home.

Several totally distinct, isolated populations of chinook salmon are spread throughout the world. In their native range along the West Coast of North America, they can be caught in three very different types of environments: wide-open ocean, tidal bays and estuaries, and large, free-running rivers that extend as far inland as the Idaho. In the non-native Great Lakes region, they are caught in the large lakes down deep, or in the various rivers and streams that feed the lakes. Beyond that, there are also populations in South America and New Zealand, and New Zealand chinook have been reproducing successfully for nearly 120 years.

In the open ocean and in the mouths of giant rivers, such as the Columbia or Kenai, trolling is the most popular method, and lures, spinners, spoons and live bait are all used effectively. Employing casted and retrieved lures in the ocean from boat, kayak, or shore is also viable, but it's a bit trickier, and the spot must be just right. While many anglers love catching chinook in the sea, the most obsessed anglers are those who hunt them in the rivers and streams. The ability to catch a giant ocean-going trout (which salmon essentially are) while wading in a beautiful, free-flowing river is what makes chinook—and other salmon and steelhead—so special. And unlike steelhead—which can often feel like hunting unicorns—catching a handful of 15- to 30-pound (7 to 14 kg) kings each day is a real possibility when they are running upriver.

The tricky thing about fishing for river chinook (or any salmon) is that they don't actively feed. They are there for one purpose: to spawn. Though anglers love to argue about the fact, biologists have shown that salmon do not digest anything once they swim inland beyond the reaches of the tides. So then, how does anyone catch them—why do they bite? There are several theories, but most agree that they strike out of instinct or aggression. Therefore, they will hit lures, flies, and even bait simply because that's what they've evolved to do. This does make it a bit tricky, and the traditional tactics of using something that looks like a bug or a minnow doesn't always work—sometimes it requires an aggressive, brash lure or fly to get the fish angry or interested enough to strike. If that isn't working, many anglers swear by cured salmon eggs as bait—there's no doubt that this is one of the most effective methods of getting the fish to take a hook under a float.

# COHO SALMON

|  | · 20 POUNDS (9 KG) · |
|---|---|
| **DIFFICULTY** | **TROPHY SIZE** |

| | |
|---|---|
| **PERFECT SPOT** | Egegik River, United States; Skeena River, Canada |
| **PREFERRED HABITAT** | Coho spend most of their time in the open sea where they can be caught close to shore with an optimum water temperature of 50 to 60°F (10 to 15°C). When they run up rivers to spawn in fall, they occupy current seams and holes in places they can hide from predators. |
| **SEASON** | Coho live for years in the ocean and can be caught year-round. The spawning run starts in fall (region specific) and river fish can be caught through winter. |
| **TOP TECHNIQUE** | Coho in open waters (ocean or lake) are mostly caught with trolling gear. In the rivers, fly fishing and centerpin fishing is the choice of the most obsessed anglers. |
| **AVERAGE SIZE** | 8 to 12 pounds (4 to 5 kg) |
| **RECORD SIZE LOCATION & DATE** | 33 pounds 4 ounces (15 kg); Pulaski, New York, United States. |

## COHO ARE THE QUINTESSENTIAL SALMON. FIVE DIFFERENT

native salmon species can be found along the Pacific coast of North America (from California through Alaska), but the coho is the most popular. They are right in the middle in terms of size—not as large as the chinook or chum, but larger than the pink or sockeye. Their physical appearance is also very similar to chinook, chum salmon, and steelhead. In the ocean and early in their freshwater migration, they are bright chrome along their flanks, with darker dorsal sides, and wide broom tails. The coho is smaller than its cousin the chinook, most often maxing out at around 20 pounds (9 kg), but its proportions are typically a bit taller and thicker in body shape. Coho lack the dark gums of the chinook, and their very clean, highly polished appearance has given them the nickname "silvers." Late in their spawning migration, as their bodies break down and they enter the final stages of their lives, they turn starkly contrasted dark brown and bright red.

Coho spend most of their lives in the open sea, and trolling in the Pacific is a popular way to catch these hard-fighting fish. That said, many of the most dedicated coho anglers are fly fishermen, who will travel great distances to specifically catch these majestic, super-charged fighting fish as they run up rivers to spawn. Anglers are known to save up their vacation time, leave the rest of the world behind, and live out of their trucks in pursuit of the coho, chinook, and steelhead (whose seasons overlap). The arrival of the anglers is a form of migration, just like the fish, and important for the local economies surrounding their home rivers. Anglers will spend dozens—or hundreds—of hours walking the banks, plying the waters, and wandering in the woods looking for the best secret spots and the largest fish. The most obsessed of these anglers will even take up seasonal work and quit when it's the peak of the salmon season.

While they are native to the Pacific coast, also like chinook and steelhead, there is a population that has been introduced to the Great Lakes region of North America. While there are some reproducing fish, the fishery is primarily sustained through stocking. These introduced fish are caught in a couple different ways, but most anglers will troll the open waters. While trolling, anglers will utilize a variety of spoons and swimming lures that mimic herring and other common baits. When coho do make their spawning run into the river tributaries of the large lakes in fall, they are a favorite target of fly anglers from all over the world. The numbers are high, and there is less ground to cover than along the Pacific coast—and the fish fight just as hard.

But it's not just trolling and fly fishermen and -women who adore these fish: those who practice centerpin fishing often are equally as obsessed. This technique is at least 150 years old and harkens back to the very first fishing reels ever developed in Europe. In centerpin fishing, the angler uses a long, soft rod, in excess of 12 feet (3.7 m), and a large arbor reel (reminiscent of a large fly reel) that has a 1:1 ratio for every turn of the handle—the spool turns one revolution; there are no gears. Using a float the angler back drifts baited hooks downstream with the current. It then naturally finds its way into seams, eddies, and pockets where the fish are. The centerpin reel is critical for this, as it puts no drag on the bait, and allows the eggs or other small bait to drift extremely naturally to where the fish are lying in ambush. It is a beloved and highly effective method that can also be hellacious—there's no drag on these reels. Using the soft action of the rods as shock absorbers, it's up to the angler to palm the reel when a fish is hooked to slow it down, which is no small feat.

# CUTTHROAT

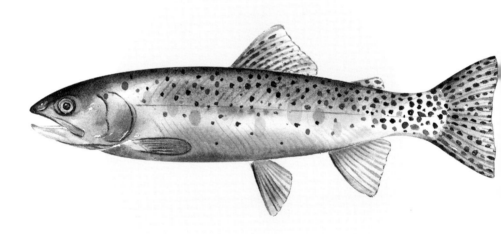

| DIFFICULTY | · 15 TO 30 INCHES (38 TO 76 CM); REGION SPECIFIC · |
| --- | --- |
| | TROPHY SIZE |

| PERFECT SPOT | Puget Sound, Washington, United States; Yellowstone River, Montana, United States |
| --- | --- |
| PREFERRED HABITAT | Cutthroat have a diverse spectrum of waters they inhabit, based on their strain. This can include small streams and creeks, large rivers, cold-water lakes, and even inland tidal waters with optimum temperatures of 45 to 65°F (7 to 18°C). |
| SEASON | Cutthroat are caught throughout the year, based on location and strain. |
| TOP TECHNIQUE | Fly fishermen and -women absolutely love cutthroat, and there is nothing like tackling them with dry flies in headwater streams, streamers in a high elevation lake, or jig flies in the salty waters of Puget Sound. |
| AVERAGE SIZE | 8 to 20 inches (20 to 51 cm); region specific |
| RECORD SIZE LOCATION & DATE | 41 pounds (19 kg); Nevada, United States, 1925 |

## CUTTHROAT ARE THE DO ALL, BE ALL, AND THRIVE ANYWHERE

native trout of Western North America. The cutthroat, or "cutties," get their name from 2 blood-red slashes that run from their chin back toward their gill plates. They are stocky, tubular, and powerfully built, with gaping maws that extend beyond their eye, and open extra wide. Cutties are adept at handling swift moving currents and are particularly astute at chasing down and consuming a wide spectrum of prey. Besides the universal hallmark slashes, they vary wildly in coloration, coming in a variety of shades, often mostly muted yellow or brown, but also dark red and even bright silver, with a various number and concentration of spots. They vary even more widely in size, and adults range from 4 to over 40 inches (10 cm to 1 m), depending on the strain and the body of water they are living in.

Cutthroat are differentiated into 10 different strains, similar to browns and rainbows. Each varies dramatically not just in size and coloration, but also in behavior. These variations—and their wide geographic distribution—have given the cutthroat extremely wide appeal to a diverse spectrum of anglers. In essence, the cutthroat is another species that can be whatever the angler enjoys best. For example, the behemoth Lahontan strain (also known sometimes as the Pyramid Lake strain) can exceed 40 pounds (18 kg), and in the large lakes and rivers it prowls, it requires the angler to fish long hours with rugged gear and perform lots of blind casting with big flies. On the other end of the spectrum, the increasingly rare Yellowstone strain is skittish as cutthroat go, but it eagerly takes dry flies in riffles at twilight in some of the most iconic rivers in the world. Other strains include the Snake River, Rio Grande, Greenback, Colorado River, Bonneville, and Paiute, but the 2 specific strains that get the highest praise, and inspire the most passion, are the westslope and the Pacific.

Westslope cutties, often known simply as "westslopes," are found throughout Western Canada and the Northwest United States. They are primarily relegated to smaller streams and headwater lakes at high elevations and in isolated areas. Westslopes are some of the smallest cuties but are beloved for where they lead anglers. Pursuit of westslopes takes anglers into pure stretches of remote, pristine wilderness. Particularly in mountain lakes and spring-fed headwaters, anglers can still catch a glimpse of what fishing was like before development and the industrial age changed everything.

Along the coast, the Pacific strain (also known as the coastal strain) is so different that it's hard to believe they are the same species. They start out life in rivers and streams, but are anadromous and head to the sea for most of their lives, moving freely between tidal, brackish, and freshwater in pursuit of feeding opportunities. They use the mighty tidal currents to their advantage, hunting shrimp and fish and grow relatively bulky and muscular compared to their small-stream cousins. They are used to chasing their prey, and as such are even more aggressive, filled with moxie, and will track down flies from a distance. Anglers absolutely adore the Pacific variation because they fight like a hurricane: with power, fury, and chaos.

Regardless of strain, all wild cutthroats are known for their bold, insolent aggression. Among the various species of trout, the cutthroat could be considered the angriest and most pugnacious. It is this quality of the cuttie that draws the most smiles, and some of the deepest feelings among anglers. They are poetry in motion, a perfectly proportioned combination of grace and violence. They are also not a difficult trout to fool; they can be so easy to catch with bait, such as worms, that artificials (and even single hooks) are the only legal method allowed in most places. This extreme aggression also means they are a fly rodder's dream. With a bit of study and some grit on the angler's part, nearly any cutthroat can be caught.

# GRAYLING

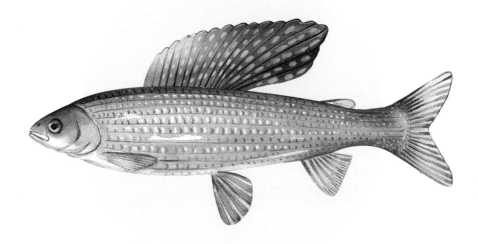

| | |
|---|---|
|  **DIFFICULTY** | **· 8 TO 20 INCHES (20 TO 51 CM);**<br>**SPECIES AND REGION SPECIFIC ·**<br>**TROPHY SIZE** |

| | |
|---|---|
| **PERFECT SPOT** | Khar Us Lake, Mongolia;<br>Lake Clark National Park, Alaska, United States |
| **PREFERRED HABITAT** | Grayling need water lower than 60°F (16°C) degrees to thrive, and are generally found in clear, clean flowing waters. They associate with current and structure in a way that allows them to catch food as it flows by. |
| **SEASON** | Grayling can be caught year-round, but many anglers focus on spring when they move into smaller streams from their overwintering lakes and large rivers. |
| **TOP TECHNIQUE** | Fly fishing is the most popular way to catch grayling, due to their small mouths and relatively small size. Dry flies can work, but small streamers and jig-like flies work best. |
| **AVERAGE SIZE** | 4 to 15 inches (3 to 38 cm); species and region specific |
| **RECORD SIZE LOCATION & DATE** | Arctic grayling: 5 pounds 15 ounces (2.7 kg);<br>Katseyedie River, Canada, 1967 |

## GRAYLING ARE THE SMALLER, MORE EXOTIC COUSINS OF

salmon and trout. There are between 13 and 15 species, which scientists are still trying to delineate. They are found throughout the colder parts of the Northern Hemisphere primarily in streams and rivers, with a few exceptions for pristine, deep lakes. Grayling appear very trout-like but there are several important distinctions. The first and most obvious is the huge dorsal sail, which is a very large fin that can be raised or lowered. These fins are often covered in beautiful markings, and give the grayling its signature, dramatic look. Grayling are also covered in larger scales than trout, and this wraps them in a striking shimmer as bright sunshine reflects off their flanks. Grayling also have small mouths—much smaller than most trout—which lends the appearance of a small head and face. Otherwise, their proportions are very trout-like, and tubular, with large, strong tails that make them highly adept at surviving in swift-moving water. Grayling are also very slow growers, and live a long time compared to trout: they may grow 1 inch (2.5 cm) a year once they reach maturity and reach 20 years old.

The Arctic grayling is the only species native to North America, and it is one of the most supremely striking and beautiful of all species. Their signature sail is dramatic—taller than their body and darkly shaded with tropical-colored turquoise stripes. These fish are common west of the Hudson Bay in Canada, and they are the most widely distributed game fish in Alaska. They were once common in the Great Lakes but were extirpated through overfishing and habitat destruction. A small wild population still exists in Montana, but they have since been reintroduced through stocking, and after nearly 100 years missing, they are now catchable again in Michigan.

The European grayling has a similar story as the Arctic grayling. It is the only native grayling in Europe and found throughout the less populated northern regions in cold, pristine water. Both the Arctic and European grayling are small fish that are relatively easy to catch with the proper tackle, and anglers cite them as one of their favorites of any fish on the planet. Expeditions to find and catch wild grayling will take anglers into wilderness that includes caribou and grizzly bears, sometimes where there are no roads or towns. There are still places in this world that are rarely, if ever, fished by modern man—much of it the stronghold of the Arctic grayling.

The Mongolian grayling typifies this point. It is a monster among its brethren, and lives only in remote locations in the Altai mountains of Mongolia. It is the biggest grayling, nearly double in size of many other species, with a wide mouth (compared to other graylings) and a huge, powerful forked tail, and large eyes. In many ways, it resembles a lake trout, and it is a powerful apex predator that can be found only in landlocked rivers—it is the only naturally occurring landlocked species of grayling. It is a rare fish, and highly respected and prized within its native waters. It has grown larger than other graylings because there are no other apex predators to compete with. Few anglers have had the opportunity to pursue these fish, but for those that have it is a life-changing experience.

If you are set to strike out your own grayling quest, pursuing them on the fly rod is the most rewarding method. Fly fishermen and -women adore the grayling, as they eat small forage that are best replicated with a fly (versus a lure), and soft fly rods are the best tool for preventing a pulled hook. They are, on average, similar in size to brook trout and landlocked rainbows, so light rods make them more fun too. That said, they are every bit as aggressive, and many argue that, pound for pound, they fight harder than most trout. But if you're not a fly angler, they're still great game fish; they will pounce on spoons, jigs, and (where legal) the same live baits you would use for small trout.

# RAINBOW TROUT

· 20 INCHES (51 CM) ·

TROPHY SIZE

| | |
|---|---|
| **PERFECT SPOT** | Madison River, United States; Kamchatka River, Russia |
| **PREFERRED HABITAT** | Rainbows are river and stream fish that need cold, clear, clean waters to survive with an optimum water temperature of 45 to 65°F (7 to 18°C). They use current to their advantage and eat a wide variety of prey. |
| **SEASON** | Rainbows feed most aggressively in spring and fall but can be caught year-round (even through ice). |
| **TOP TECHNIQUE** | Fly fishing for wild rainbows with dry flies is one of the most rewarding types of fishing, bar none. Streamers and nymph flies are also beloved. However, rainbows can be caught using simple baits like worms and crickets, and as with bass and panfish, lures such as crank baits and spinners. |
| **AVERAGE SIZE** | 6 to 15 inches (15 to 38 cm) |
| **RECORD SIZE LOCATION & DATE** | 48 pounds (22 kg), 42 inches (1 m); Lake Diefenbaker, Canada, 2009 |

# RAINBOWS ARE THE TROUT BY WHICH ALL OTHERS ARE

compared and the most widely distributed trout worldwide. They are found in every corner of North America and on every continent in the world (besides Antarctica). Their far-flung distribution is no mistake—humans have sprinkled them across the world because they are an amazing, beloved game fish. While they fight hard and are rewarding on the end of the line, it is the way they feed that draws in most anglers. It feels like it is an embodiment of Mother Nature herself, and watching a rainbow rise to a fly is a sanctified moment for so many anglers.

Rainbows are built for the river: thick tubular bodies, a broad, fanlike tail, a typically proportioned mouth, and bright eyes that glimmer with cagey cunning. They are a strikingly colorful trout with an intense density of jet-black spots set against an iridescent flank of off-yellow, light green, and a broad, bright swatch of dark pink (where they get their name). Rainbows are native to the coastlines of the Pacific Ocean, from the Baja of California to Alaska, and from the northern coastal edges of China through Russia to Siberia. They are a cold-water fish, primarily found in rivers and streams, and require highly oxygenated and clean waters to survive.

Like brown trout, many strains or subspecies of rainbows are named after the waterways in which they inhabit (e.g., Eagle Lake, Kern River, Rio Mayo, etc.). Each has differences in biology and behavior; including what they most commonly eat, how they behave, and how fast they grow. Rainbows can act and look markedly different throughout the world, and this diversity is mirrored perfectly by the diversity of anglers that pursue them. From a kid with a bobber and a worm in New York, to the dry fly aficionado in KwaZulu-Natal, South Africa, to the farmer with a homemade spoon in Kamchatka, Russia, the rainbow is the trout that unites anglers of all walks of life under one banner.

Truly, the rainbow might be responsible for more memories and fulfilling days on the water than any other fish—even the sunfish or bass.

Rainbows are in harmony with the cycles of the river and rely heavily on aquatic insects for food. Mayflies, stoneflies, and dragonflies live underwater alongside rainbows for much of their lives (where they're called nymphs), only crawling out of the water and morphing into aerial forms as they fully mature. They then breed and deposit eggs back in the water, and the cycle continues. Rainbows eat these insects at all stages, but particularly rely on them as they "hatch" or "emerge," whereby they come out from their hiding places and move toward the surface. As they climb, float, and swim they become vulnerable. Rainbows are renowned for becoming hypnotized by a specific insect, ignoring all other prey. It's a predation strategy that helps them identify, target, and snatch up small, fast-moving prey as it zips by in the current. Therein lies one of the puzzles of fishing for rainbows: you must mimic the bug they're feeding on perfectly, or risk leaving the river defeated.

Fly anglers will study their local waters and determine when certain insects are most likely to emerge and come to the river armed with small boxes of custom, self-tied flies mimicking every bug imaginable, hoping to be prepared. Then, it's a game of observation and patience. After trying desperately for an hour to mimic an insect with a dozen miniscule number 22 dry flies (that probably look nearly identical to the fishermen and -women), to finally see a rainbow take the fly, get hooked, and erupt out of the water in a dramatic leap is a triumph of the highest order in angling. The goosebumps and butterflies that come with that moment cannot be overstated. It is the moment anglers dream about, and the thought that gets them through every business meeting or traffic jam. For wild trout fishermen and -women, it is the pinnacle of angling glory.

RIVERS AND STREAMS

# STEELHEAD

| | |
|---|---|
| **DIFFICULTY** | **· 40 INCHES (1 M) ·**<br>**TROPHY SIZE** |

| | |
|---|---|
| **PERFECT SPOT** | Umpqua River, United States; Situk River, United States |
| **PREFERRED HABITAT** | Found in large tidal rivers and associate with structure and current like other trout, but often like the slower, flatter sections; optimum water temperature is 45 to 55°F (7 to 12°C) though it varies by season and region. |
| **SEASON** | Depending on the river, steelhead can be present year-round. The summer run starts in midsummer (June and July) and ends in late winter (February and March), and the winter run usually starts around December and ends by March. |
| **TOP TECHNIQUE** | Many anglers prefer to catch steelhead with a fly rod and streamers, but they can be caught with a variety of methods including casting lures and using bait with centerpin rods and reels. |
| **AVERAGE SIZE** | 30 to 35 inches (76 to 89 cm) |
| **RECORD SIZE LOCATION & DATE** | Since steelhead are technically not their own species, there is no world record; however, fish over 30 pounds (14 kg) and 45 inches (1.1 m) have been documented. |

## STEELHEAD ARE NOT ACTUALLY A DISTINCT SPECIES;

technically, they're "just" rainbow trout, right down to their DNA. What sets steelhead apart is a magical behavior. While rainbows stay within a river their whole lives, something switches for a steelhead at around 3 years old. They turn silver and bright, abandon the freshwater of their youth, and head out into the immensity of the Pacific Ocean. There, they live for years, contending with sharks and whales, and transforming into chrome torpedoes, bulking up, while developing a vicious attitude.

In their native range, steelhead make two yearly spawning runs, constituted by different populations of fish. The "summer fish" mature during their lengthy 3- to 6-month travels (hundreds of miles) inland to their preferred spawning habitats. The "winter fish" arrive very late in the year, are fully mature, and may spawn within a couple days, often close to the ocean—their run is much shorter, often less than 6 weeks. Winter and summer fish are genetically distinct, having specific mutations that split them into one behavior or the other. But because they do not die after spawning, steelhead can make their journey several times in their lives and stay hungry and vigorous throughout the process. With the summer and winter fish almost constantly coming and going, anglers can chase them year-round.

Steelhead are native to large tidal rivers west of the Rockies, but they were introduced to the Great Lakes around the turn of the twentieth century. Now well established, these big fish run from the huge freshwater lakes into river and stream tributaries to spawn. It's a totally freshwater version of the West Coast sea-run behavior. This East Coast fishery has developed nearly as devoted a following as the native run out West, with anglers traveling from around the world to fish the spawning runs in the colder months of the year.

Anglers who fish for "steelies" employ two methods commonly used for salmon—the center-pin float, and the wet-fly swing. There are certainly anglers who use traditional spinning gear or one-handed fly rods (especially in the East), but they are in the minority. Steelhead bring their aggressive attitudes into rivers, but they are stubborn and will typically not chase a fly very far—only 1 or 2 feet (30 to 61 cm) from their holding position. Centerpin—as described in the coho profile—helps cover every inch of the river, but with the fly, anglers must employ a meticulous pattern of presentation. The process starts by casting up and across the current, and then letting the fly swing with the current in an arc until it's virtually straight downstream. The angler then strips it back in, takes three steps down current, and then does it all again. This is repeated for a few yards or a few miles depending on the river, the structure, and the angler's determination. This method ensures the fly swings through every inch of the steelhead's path, even if it's unwilling to chase.

Particularly out West, the scenery surrounding many steelhead waters is postcard perfection. These are some of the wildest, most pristine places in the world. For so many anglers, this is why they can spend an inordinate amount of time—often days and weeks straight—repeating the same casting motions for just a handful of fish. Standing in a river as clear as glass, surrounded by a rugged, pristine mountainous landscape, hunting fish powered by a life at sea, is a visceral experience.

The steelhead attracts a very hard-core, fanatically obsessed group of anglers who live and breathe these fish. Some might say that "steelheaders" are the pinnacle of the cliché trout bum, and it's certainly true that many rearrange their entire lives to chase these fish. There is something special, and intangible, about the steelhead that flips the addiction switch. It could be their size, their fussy-but-savage nature, or the wild places in which they live, but most anglers will tell you it's something more. They will tell you it's just something you have to experience, and feel for yourself, and then you'll know.

# STURGEON

| | |
|---|---|
| **DIFFICULTY** | **· OVER 6 FEET LONG (1.8 M) ·**<br>**TROPHY SIZE** |

| | |
|---|---|
| **PERFECT SPOT** | Columbia River, Washington, United States;<br>Fraser River, British Columbia, Canada |
| **PREFERRED HABITAT** | White sturgeon move between the Pacific Ocean and large coastal rivers. They can be found feeding in faster, deeper sections of rivers with an optimum water temperature of 50 to 65°F (10 to 18°C). |
| **SEASON** | White sturgeon can be caught throughout the year (depending on the region). |
| **TOP TECHNIQUE** | Live bait fished on the bottom is the technique used to catch these fish. Popular baits include worms, shad, and shrimp. Heavy weight is required to keep it on the bottom in strong currents. |
| **AVERAGE SIZE** | 3 to 6 feet long (91 to 183 cm) |
| **RECORD SIZE LOCATION & DATE** | 468 pounds (212 kg);<br>California, United States, 1983<br>Note: It is no longer legal to pursue records for white sturgeon. |

# NO OTHER FISH WILL BE MISTAKEN FOR A STURGEON. THEY

are supremely unique, with elongated brown-gray bodies laced with blade-like ridges (called scutes) running along their dorsal and flank. These rock-hard plates are extremely sharp and offer the fish protection from predators and will slice the hand of an unwary angler. Sturgeon also have large pectoral fins that are permanently affixed out from their bodies, and a dorsal fin that is so far back on the body it nearly attaches to the large, forked, tail. Sturgeon have an angular head and a large nose called a rostrum with a downward facing mouth and 4 barbels that protrude down and forward, used for finding food as they scrounge along the bottom. Unlike any other fish in this book, sturgeon do not have a spine—they are almost entirely made of cartilage. To say they are unique is an understatement.

There are 28 species of sturgeon throughout the world that all look very similar, and most get large. The white sturgeon is the largest freshwater fish in North America, and the beluga sturgeon is the largest freshwater fish anywhere in the world (and is found in Russia). White sturgeon are also one of the most popular and premier game fish in the rivers and estuaries of the Pacific Northwest of North America. There are many white sturgeon caught each year in excess of 7 feet (2.1 m) and several hundred pounds, but they are rumored to reach nearly 20 feet (6 m) long and almost 2,000 pounds (907 kg), with confirmed fish captured by biologists measuring nearly 15 feet (4.5 m) and over 1,500 pounds (684)! These fish are also old—sturgeon don't even reach maturity until at least 10 to 20 years, and they are known to live over 100 years.

Sturgeon are often called "dinosaurs" because of their prehistoric appearance. They survived the great extinction event that wiped out 90 percent of animals on Earth, and have existed in their current form for nearly 200 million years. This makes them one of the oldest-surviving animals on the planet. Their ancient evolution, gigantic size, and long-lived nature give them the reputation as the soul of the rivers they live in. White sturgeon almost went extinct after overexploitation by frontier settlers, and then they struggled to exist with the damming of their critical spawning rivers and the demand for caviar (salted, unfertilized sturgeon eggs). However, with the evolution of more protective management measures over the last 100 years, and the removal of more and more dams, white sturgeon have rebounded and now offer anglers reliable, exceptional angling opportunities.

Sturgeon have an excellent sense of smell but very poor eyesight, so anglers pursue them with bait, which differs by region—it can be anything from nightcrawlers to full-size dead shad to chunks of lamprey. Sturgeon experts hunt for reliable places in the river that these fish frequent, with the largest fish often caught near tailwaters that have a lot of current. Sturgeon are so strong and efficiently built there is no current they can't easily power through. They use this to their advantage to cruise the bottom vacuuming up prey that can't escape. To get the bait down requires using heavy weights—anglers often use sinkers weighing over 1 pound (0.5 kg). These massive sinkers, hard-running currents, and gigantic fish require very strong, specialized tackle. Most anglers use main lines of 50 to 80 pounds (23 to 36 kg), and very heavy leaders with large gauge circle hooks.

When they get large, sturgeons become extremely strong fighters. It's an endurance game that can take hours and a whole team of anglers trying to subdue a trophy-sized 500-plus-pound (227 kg) fish. While they primarily dog the angler with heavy, ruthless pressure, they will make hard runs repeatedly away from the boat. And while it doesn't happen every time, anglers are sometimes treated to a spectacle: Giant white sturgeon will jump when hooked. Seeing an 8-foot-long (2.4 m) fish that looks like a dinosaur explode from the surface of a freshwater river is a surreal, exhilarating moment that can change an angler forever.

# SALTWATER FISH

# BLACK AND
# BLUE ROCKFISH

|  | · 6 POUNDS (2.7 KG) · |
|---|---|
| **DIFFICULTY** | **TROPHY SIZE** |

| | |
|---|---|
| **PERFECT SPOT** | Pacific City, Oregon, United States; Kenai Peninsula, Alaska, United States |
| **PREFERRED HABITAT** | While most rockfish are deep water species, blacks and blues can be caught in a huge spectrum of depths. They are often found around rocky outcrops and ledges, as well as kelp forests, jetties, and tidal current lines. |
| **SEASON** | Due to the rugged and cold waters these fish are found in, summer is the best time to pursue them. |
| **TOP TECHNIQUE** | Most anglers will drop bait down deep, but many will agree the most fun way to catch blacks and blues is casting lures. Swimbaits are very popular. |
| **AVERAGE SIZE** | 1 to 3 pounds (0.5 to 1.4 kg); black rockfish tend to be heavier than blue rockfish |
| **RECORD SIZE LOCATION & DATE** | Black rockfish: 13 pounds 5 ounces (6 kg); Gulf of Alaska, Alaska, United States, 2005 Blue rockfish: 8 pounds 6 ounces (4 kg); Whaler's Cove, Alaska, United States, 1994 |

## OUT OF DOZENS OF SPECIES, BLACK ROCKFISH AND BLUE

rockfish are the two most popular rockfish species of the Pacific coast. Blacks and blues are very hard to tell apart, having nearly identical body shapes, and freshwater anglers will find them strikingly similar to largemouth bass. Their bodies are thick and robust, and oval shaped, with a broad tail and large pectoral fins. Their dorsal fin is prominent when erect, and it has sinister, piercing spikes that protect the fish from being eaten by predators. Both species have enlarged eyes, with the blue rockfish having theirs slightly pushed forward. Both species are demurely and darkly colored, with some speckling of lighter and darker banding and patterning.

Blacks and blues can be found from Southern California through the Alaskan coastline, from right in tight to shore to many miles out into the sea. These fish are generally associated with the continental shelf and, like other rockfish, are often pursued in deep or very deep waters, between 200 and 1,200 feet (61 to 366 m), where there is significant rocky structure or kelp forests. Unlike most other rockfish that can only be exclusively caught in deep water near the bottom, both blues and blacks can be caught in the upper portions of the water column. In many places, they also are known to feed right on the surface and come close to shore where they can be caught from jetties and rocky outcrops.

Most anglers love catching rockfish because once you find the fish, it's fast action and you can expect hits on every cast. These two species are particularly beloved because while most rockfish species don't fight much, blacks and blues take drag and pull hard. They can be cast to with lures, too, since they often stay shallow, and this makes the fishing more engaging than just dropping baits down extremely deep. There are even times they will "blitz" on or near the surface, attacking schools of bait in a frenzy, jumping out of the water and making a lot of commotion. Even fly-fishers and kayakers can get in on the action when these scrappy fish hit the surface.

The type of fishing that is most unique to blues and blacks is dory fishing. Along a slice of the Pacific Northwest coast, there are very few ramps to launch a boat because of the sheer, rugged, rocky shorelines. For decades, intrepid anglers have solved this problem by directly launching from the limited sandy beaches that dot the shorelines. It's a rugged, sometimes harrowing launch where a duo of anglers uses a heavy-duty truck to quickly back the specially designed dories into the surf line, shooting the boat into the water. These boats are durable and are built to take on the surf launch, but the landing is perhaps even more dramatic. Dory anglers will run at the beach and hit the sand at full speed. This will launch the rugged boats far enough up the sand that they can be towed away from the breaking waves. The level of dedication these anglers have for the rockfish drives them to take on this harrowing and traditional method of getting to the fishing grounds.

When they are not on the surface, anglers generally pursue blues and blacks with heavy sinkers, multiple hooks, and bait rigged on dropper loops. Various different cut baits can be used, and when these fish are feeding, most anything will work. Many anglers swear by squid and octopus. Live bait is far from the only thing that anglers use in pursuit of these feisty fish, and many lures can be used if they can get down to the fish. Bladed jigs are very popular, as are soft plastic swimbaits on heavy jig heads. The swimbait and jig are especially effective when the fish are near the surface or close to shore, and they are likely the preferred method if they can be employed.

# BONEFISH

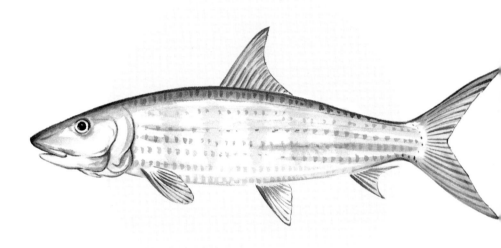

|  | · OVER 10 POUNDS (5 KG); 28 INCHES (71 CM) · |
|:---:|:---:|
| **DIFFICULTY** | **TROPHY SIZE** |

| | |
|---:|:---|
| **PERFECT SPOT** | Andros Island, Bahamas; Seychelles |
| **PREFERRED HABITAT** | Pristine tropical flats, including grass beds and coral shoals, adjacent to deep water. Often found hunting for mollusks and crustaceans in very shallow water; optimum water temperature is 70 to 85°F (21 to 29°C). |
| **SEASON** | They are found year-round in tropical and subtropical locations. |
| **TOP TECHNIQUE** | Small jigs and soft plastics are effective, but fly fishing for bonefish is considered a top art. Use small shrimp and crab patterns that match the locally available forage. |
| **AVERAGE SIZE** | 15 to 20 inches (38 to 51 cm) |
| **RECORD SIZE LOCATION & DATE** | 16 pounds (7 kg), 34 inches (85 cm); Bimini, Bahamas, 1971 |

## THE BONEFISH IS A FISH WITH A DIVINE, SUPERNATURAL

reputation. It has a body that appears made entirely of tiny, seamless mirrors. Even its eye is silver and reflective around the large, jet-black pupil. Glassy, reflective scales, with a subtle gray overtone, are the ultimate camouflage allowing them to blend into their environment of crystalline water over sandy and light-colored bottoms. They are intensely hard to see and disappear in plain sight like wisps of smoke. This trait has earned them the moniker "ghosts of the flats." Like ethereal spirits, they can appear seemingly from nowhere, and then in a flash are gone again, dissolving into the background or exploding away in dramatic sprint that end at the horizon.

Bonefish are an ancient fish, perhaps 150 million years old; they swim in the same waters today as they did in the time of the dinosaurs. The bonefish is a creature of many mysteries. Among them are where and how they spawn, where the juveniles feed and grow up, and their general life cycle thereafter. They are a relatively new target for sport anglers, having largely been ignored until the 1940s (the first "official" fly-caught bonefish was 1939), but then exploding in popularity in the 1970s, and continuing to today.

"Bones" are found only in the cleanest, clearest, and warmest tropical and subtropical waters of the world. There are at least 11 different species, though they all look virtually identical. They spend much of their non-feeding time in deep waters (hundreds of feet deep), but mature bones slide onto shallow flats with the rising tide where they hunt small crustaceans and mollusks (shrimp, crabs, and snails). Yet even when they are close and clearly visible, bones are one of the most frustrating and formidable fish to actually hook. Indeed, bones are arguably the wariest, most skittish gamefish in the world. They evolved to flee at maximum speed at the merest hint of danger, because of their vulnerability in their shallow-water feeding grounds. They can spook from the distant echo of a subtle hull slap from a flat's skiff, a single wrong footfall of a wading angler, or even the shadow of a fly line in the air. And these are the fish that anglers see—many are never seen, as they don't come close enough to be noticed. Anglers may fish with highly skilled guides for days on end, spot many, but only get a handful of shots—landing just a couple in a day is considered amazing success.

In addition to the allure of hunting an ultra-elusive fish in super-skinny water, anglers cherish bonefish for their speed. They have deeply, exceptionally forked tails similar to what is found on a pelagic species like a swordfish or tuna. While many inshore fish can achieve bursts of speed, bonefish can explode into 30-mile-per-hour (48 km/h) runs that they can maintain for long distances. An angler who hooks their first bonefish will be shocked how the fish goes from being 30 feet (9 m) in front of them to 100 yards (91 m) away in a mere blink.

There are plenty of anglers who cast small jigs and soft plastics to bones (or even live shrimp), and this is an effective but still challenging method to catch them. But the popularity of this mythical speedster has gone hand in hand with the increase in popularity of saltwater fly fishing. Indeed, the bonefish is one of the most impactful species in the rise and development of many sight fishing techniques, which have crossed over to fishing for everything from redfish to carp. There is no doubt that catching bones is a supreme challenge, and those who fish for bonefish do so with fixation so full of zeal that falls firmly within the sphere of absolute infatuation.

# COBIA

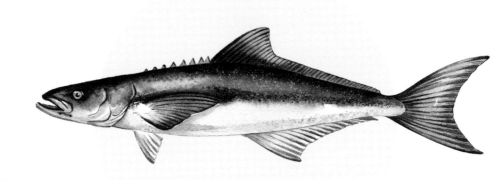

| | |
|---|---|
| **DIFFICULTY** | **· 75 POUNDS (34 KG) ·**<br>**TROPHY SIZE** |

| | |
|---|---|
| **PERFECT SPOT** | Chesapeake Bay, Virginia, United States;<br>Shark Bay, Gascoyne, Australia |
| **PREFERRED HABITAT** | Cobia can be found just about anywhere there is bait. They can be found associated with heavy structure or cruising the open ocean. Understanding when cobia move through your local waters is key; they enjoy water between 65 and 75°F (18 to 24°C). |
| **SEASON** | Year-round |
| **TOP TECHNIQUE** | Large live baits are your best bet, but sight fishing with jigs and large soft plastic lures is very popular. |
| **AVERAGE SIZE** | 15 to 50 pounds (7 to 23 kg) |
| **RECORD SIZE LOCATION & DATE** | 135 pounds 9 ounces (61 kg);<br>Shark Bay, Western Australia, 1985 |

## COBIA ARE LEGENDARY, TACKLE-BUSTING BRAWLERS. THEIR

muscular bodies are matched to a tail that is a combination of broad and forked at the same time, which in turn makes them both fast and strong. In open water they burn off tons of drag, relentlessly gunning for the horizon. But if the angler is fishing around structure, cobia will dive hard, hunting for bottom or bolting into anything they can use to break the line. They are ruthless and give 100 percent from the second they feel the hook point. Even tangling with a small, 20-pound (9 kg) cobia can be an exhausting fight, but if the angler is fortunate enough to tie into a trophy-sized fish on spinning gear, they are in for a battle.

For all their fire and fury, the cobia has a relatively drab appearance. They are dark brown on their dorsal side, often with a broad off-white stripe that runs the length of their body. They have a dorsal fin that is set far back, and their heads and the front half of their bodies are broad and flattened. Cobia appear almost catfish-like when viewed from above, but they swim with their pectoral fins out to the sides just like a shark. In fact, cobia look remarkably like sharks when they're lazily swimming along the surface, particularly from a distance.

Cobia have a huge range—which changes seasonally—extending to both sides of the Atlantic, throughout the Indian Ocean, and into the western Pacific. They perfectly straddle the line between being an inshore, structure-oriented fish, and a blue water, pelagic fish. They are just as likely to be found in very shallow water, tight to shore, as they are 50 or more miles (80 km) offshore in deep water. In some offshore spots, they can be pinned to the bottom in holes, or hanging over humps or wrecks. In other places, they will simply be cruising in the open, right on the surface, or associating with floating debris or vegetation. They are highly adaptable, curious, and brash, but also wary and cunning—the cobia has a knack for suddenly showing up out of nowhere and disappearing just as quickly.

Cobia are rarely found in schools. However, they do like company, and they often tag along with large sea creatures such as giant stingrays, sharks, turtles, and even whales. They do this to take advantage of the cover the larger animal provides, but also because larger animals spook bait, causing it to panic and flee, becoming vulnerable. Many captains suggest keeping an eye out for larger animals, and even if you can't see a cobia with it, consider taking a careful cast around it.

Though they have been caught using virtually every method, cobia are generally pursued with either large live baits or jigs. With their broad mouths, these fish will hammer giant baits—whole menhaden or bluefish pitched on heavy tackle are attacked with reckless savagery. Live eels are another extremely popular bait for cobia, and there is no such thing as too big; they will suck down a 20-inch (51 cm) eel in the blink of an eye. Cobia feed at all levels of the water column, and anglers fishing heavy structures—such as wrecks or reefs—can blind cast and drop baits down to where the fish are waiting. Jigging deep can work too, but for those who choose artificials, it often goes hand in hand with sight fishing.

Sight casting for these fish is a deeply rooted passion of cobia diehards. Anglers hunt for a cobia in the endless frontier of the open ocean, often for long periods, slowly cruising and meticulously scanning the surface from high-up on a raised platform. Once a fish is spotted, maneuvering and preparing the boat for that first cast is all about precision. Then, there is the heart-pounding intensity of the first cast—often the only shot the angler will get—when the fish dives for the jig. It never gets old, and when the cobia strikes and is hooked, it always lives up to its reputation as one of the all-time great fighters.

# CORBINA

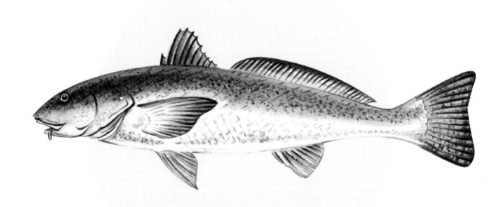

| | |
|---|---|
| <br>**DIFFICULTY** | **· OVER 3 POUNDS (1.4 KG);**<br>**20 INCHES (51 CM) ·**<br>**TROPHY SIZE** |

| | |
|---|---|
| **PERFECT SPOT** | Coronado, California, United States;<br>Cabos San Lucas, Mexico |
| **PREFERRED HABITAT** | Corbina are found along the sandy beaches from the Baja of Mexico to central California. They are typically found very tight to the beach, often in inches of water—with an optimum water temperature of 60 to 70°F (16 to 21°C)—hunting mole crabs, worms, and small baitfish. |
| **SEASON** | Corbina are caught from early summer through late fall. |
| **TOP TECHNIQUE** | By far the most popular method for catching corbina is using freshly captured mole crabs on a small hook, with as little weight as possible. Fly anglers love catching corbina too, and often use typical bonefish flies and mole crab patterns. |
| **AVERAGE SIZE** | 1 to 2 pounds (0.5 to 0.9 kg);<br>10 to 15 inches (25 to 38 cm) |
| **RECORD SIZE LOCATION & DATE** | 7 pounds 15 ounces (4 kg);<br>Mission Bay, California, United States, 2004 |

# CORBINA ARE THE ELUSIVE PHANTOMS OF THE PACIFIC SURF

line. They slide in and out of the breakers with such ease, they can be there one moment and gone the next—it's easy for anglers to mistake them for a mirage: a figment of the imagination. For this reason, they have earned the nickname "ghosts of the coast." They are relatively small, stocky fish—usually under 5 pounds (2.3 kg)—with a bit of a humped back, and wide, powerful tails. Though small, they are mighty, and they use their strength and that large tail to cut through the churn at the surf's edge. They are plainly and uniformly silver-gray, with a slightly darker dorsal side, but in the dancing-light reflecting off sparkling waves, subtle iridescent hues are traced along their sides. The hallmark of their appearance, however, are their thick lips and single barbels at the edges of the mouth. They use the barbels to find prey, and then their thick lips to "vacuum-up" their favorite foods buried or scuttling along the sandy shallows of their preferred habitat.

Corbina are ultra-shallow surf zone specialists. While they can be caught by boat, they are almost always found tight to shore using the natural ebb and flow of breaking waves to push and pull them into the surf line. Corbina risk coming in exceedingly shallow primarily to chase their favorite food, the ubiquitous mole crab—also known as the sand flea or sand crab. To hunt them, the corbina often must come in so shallow they can be seen with their backs and tails completely out of the water as they skim along receding waves.

This behavior means the corbina are within reach of anyone, but they are not a fish for everyone; corbina have a notorious reputation of being difficult to catch. Since they live most of their lives at the constantly shifting border of land and sea, the corbina must be on guard all the time. They will bolt for safety at the merest hint of danger such as a poorly placed cast, an angler wading ankle deep, or even if they detect fishing line in the water. Once they're gone, they often won't return to the spot for hours, or even a day or more. They are also wiley and fussy, and they will refuse lures or flies for seemingly no reason at all. What worked yesterday won't necessarily work today. These characteristics all contribute to their reputation, and many anglers will pass up corbina in favor of less wary and frustrating quarry. But for those that love the devilish little corbina, the pursuit and hunt is done precisely because they are so tough to catch.

While saltwater fishing typically requires extra-tough, specialized gear, corbina can be caught with basic freshwater rods and reels. Corbina aren't large fish, and since they're in so tight, there is no need to make long casts. Determined anglers often use longer, softer rods and light lines. They will dig fresh mole crabs from the sand (a beloved part of the fishing process), and fish them on very small hooks, with light weights. The long rod and thin line help cast the small crabs and light sinkers more easily, while also helping prevent pulled hooks. Corbina will fight hard and take drag against these light setups, so patience is the key, and using the waves to help land the fish is crucial.

The corbina also has skyrocketed in popularity in the last decade (or so) as a top-notch fly-fishing target. Their appetite for small prey and the ability to sight fish for these ghostlike fish strikes a chord, in the same way bonefish, trout, and carp speak to fly anglers. Sight casting to corbina (with any method) often requires a lot of stealth, observation, and patience, while waiting for the perfect moment to cast. Plus, the feisty fish pull hard once hooked, and they will rip the fly line right out of your hand when you finally hook one. There is a whole lot to obsess about in this little fish, and for many anglers, it's the fish that speaks to them more than any other.

# FLOUNDER

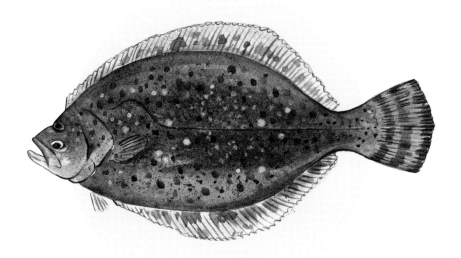

**· 5 TO 15 POUNDS (2.3 TO 7 KG);
SPECIES DEPENDENT ·**

TROPHY SIZE

| | |
|---|---|
| **PERFECT SPOT** | Ocracoke Island, United States; Matanzas Inlet, United States |
| **PREFERRED HABITAT** | Flounder are highly adaptable and found in most inshore coastal waters. |
| **SEASON** | Flounder fishing is done in warmer months when most species migrate inshore from offshore waters. |
| **TOP TECHNIQUE** | Jigging for flounder is the best method and getting a bit of bait down to the bottom is key. However, flounder will strike swimming lures and soft plastics fished near the bottom. |
| **AVERAGE SIZE** | 2 to 10 pounds (0.9 to 5 kg); species dependent |
| **RECORD SIZE LOCATION & DATE** | Summer flounder (fluke): 22 pounds 7 ounces (10 kg); New York, United States, 1975 Southern flounder: 20 pounds 9 ounces (9 kg); Florida, United States, 1983 |

## FLOUNDER IS THE MOST EASILY RECOGNIZED OF ALL GAME

fish. The 800 species in the order *Pleuronectiformes*—which includes flounder, dabs, sole, plaice, and the mighty halibut—are all marked by a very flat body shape. These species all have similar coloration too, with a very dark and often patterned "upper" side and a very lightly colored "lower" side. The dark side blends in so well with the bottom, that when a flounder lays flat on the seafloor they almost disappear. They are the ultimate ambush predator and are so compressed they virtually dissolve into the rocks or sand they lay upon.

In a dramatic example of form matching function, flounder have both eyes on one side of their head—the "upper" side that faces towards the surface. This allows them to hunt more accurately while lying flat on the bottom, affording them binocular vision they wouldn't have otherwise.

Flounder are particularly popular to catch in Japan, Australia, the countries bordering the Mediterranean Sea, and in Northern Africa. In the United States they are the most popular saltwater species according to federal statistics. There are 3 species that are most pursued on the Atlantic side of the US, where flounder fishing is likely the most popular worldwide. The summer flounder is the first and it is found up and down the coast. It's often called a "fluke," and it is caught in inshore waters. Fluke are aggressive fish that will attack anything. They are beloved because they often congregate in high concentrations, and once the angler finds a hot spot, it's easy to "limit out" in short order, and then continue catching dozens more just for fun. They are an adaptable fish that can be found in a wide spectrum of environments, from small estuaries to deep offshore shoals. They are also one of the species of flounder that will change their color based on the bottom coloration, allowing them to blend in better to their surroundings.

Farther south, both gulf flounder and southern flounder can be caught in an overlapping range. They can be found throughout the Gulf of Mexico and northward to the mid-Atlantic. Like the summer flounder, these species are adaptable, and anglers pursue them over a variety of depths and locations. The southern flounder is similar, but it is unique in its ability to survive low salinity and brackish waters and will therefore come farther into bays and up into tidal creeks and ponds. Also like the summer flounder, both the gulf and southern species can be found in heavy concentrations—finding a good spot rarely results in just a couple fish.

Despite their funny shape, all three species are armed with big, sharp teeth and a substantial mouth that can take down large prey. Flounder are far more active than anglers realize; they don't just sit still waiting for prey, but instead they will chase it down, coming farther off the bottom than one might expect. They're fast too and can sprint hard to tackle prey or escape a predator.

No matter the species, a flounder or fluke rig is a simple way to get started catching them. This usually involves two baits, with one tied in above the other. The end of the rig will have some weight and typically either a soft plastic lure or a bait strip on a jig head. Above this lower jig is another baited hook that either has no or very little weight. The upper hook can have the same or slightly different bait—sometimes having two different baits can increase the catch rate. The rig is then bounced along the bottom as the boat drifts through a likely spot, or it can be cast and slowly jigged back to the angler on shore. The key is to get down deep, without constantly dragging or snagging the bottom. Dialing in the perfect drift speed, jig weight, and type of bait can be super satisfying, and horsing up a couple dozen "flatties" is icing on the cake.

# PERMIT

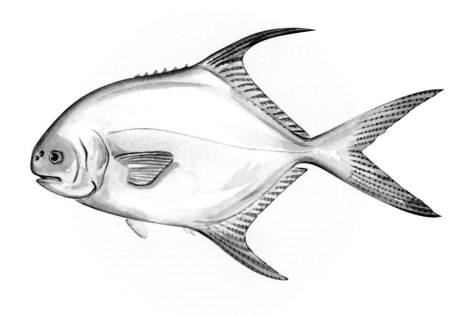

|  | · 30 POUNDS (14 KG) · |
|:---:|:---:|
| **DIFFICULTY** | **TROPHY SIZE** |

| | |
|---|---|
| **PERFECT SPOT** | Sugarloaf Key, United States; Port Honduras Marine Reserve, Belize |
| **PREFERRED HABITAT** | Permit are an inshore species that can be found from 1 to 100 feet (30 cm to 30 m) of water and prefer 70 to 80°F (21 to 27°C). In open water, they associate with structures like wrecks, but on shallow flats they cruise open areas looking for crabs and mollusks. |
| **SEASON** | Permit can be caught year-round in tropical waters. |
| **TOP TECHNIQUE** | Using a live crab is the easiest way to land a permit, though far from easy. Fly fishing for permit is seen as the pinnacle of angling throughout the world. |
| **AVERAGE SIZE** | 10 to 20 pounds (5 to 9 kg) |
| **RECORD SIZE LOCATION & DATE** | 60 pounds (27 kg); Ilha do Mel, Paranagua, Brazil, 2002 |

# PERMIT ARE A FISH THAT ANGLERS HATE TO LOVE, BUT LOVE

deeply nonetheless. They are ridiculously finicky and elusive, preposterously strong, notorious for snubbing a perfect presentation, and absurdly wary on the shallow water flats they roam. Like bonefish, they are hard to spot at any distance (even when tailing), and constantly on the move. In other words, they're nearly impossible to get to feed, and once hooked, they are nearly as hard to land. Expectation of failure is always high with permit. As a result, landing even just one is perceived as a life-fulfilling accomplishment.

Permit are in the jack family and have a similar body shape. They are compressed laterally, so they are very tall and thin; many anglers refer to them as "garbage pail lids" or "swimming sheets of plywood" because they are so flat. They are another very polished fish, with a smooth flank that is like a mirror of fine metal. One of the hallmarks of this species is their fat, fleshy lips that surround their relatively small mouths. These lips protect them as they feed on spiny and sharp prey—these fish are crab and mollusk eating specialists. Permit eyes are large and bulge slightly from the sides of their heads, and they use their vision to track prey from a distance. Yet, because of their flat body, they can't see directly in front of them when prey is close. Therefore, when they are feeding, they rely on vibration and smell in the last moments to grab their prey. This makes live bait fishing with crabs by far the easiest method to catch a permit—though not exactly easy—and makes using artificials just that much more difficult.

An exemplification of just how difficult it is to catch a permit is mostly clearly demonstrated through the experience of the angler that holds the fly-fishing world record. Del Brown—also known as "Mr. Permit"—caught the legendary 41-pound (19 kg) fish in 1992 and is known as the most dedicated permit angler of all time. Actually, he is considered one of the most dedicated anglers anywhere in the world, of any species. Permit became his fascination, and his life became totally dedicated to catching them on the flats of the Florida Keys. Through his fly innovations he changed the way anglers fish for permit, and famous anglers and guides alike have given him the highest possible praise. Yet, even this ultra-dedicated, totally obsessed angler "only" landed a little over 500 permit in his entire lifetime, and most agree that no one will ever beat that record.

While permit are hard to fool, it cannot be discounted how powerful they are once hooked. Their flat bodies allow them to put incredible pressure on the line, but their large, forked tails and muscular build also gives them speed. Getting over the hurdle of getting one to bite is just the beginning, and there can be no celebration until the fish is firmly in hand. They are notorious for burning off drag at frightening speeds, with an unrelenting endurance, and then turning their bodies sideways and resisting with a force that is hard to comprehend. And yet, somehow, during all their excessive pulling and lightning-fast running, they often work the hook loose and come off. How they can pull so hard and not stay hooked is another part of their mystery.

Most anglers assume permit can only be caught on the flats from Florida through South America, because that is where the majority are caught. However, they also can be targeted in deeper water and range as far north as the mid-Atlantic. They will associate with wrecks and substantial structure during specific times of the year and will move between deeper water and shallow water flats with regularity. That said, there truly is nothing like casting at tailing permit on the flats. Tracking and hunting one down takes fortitude and grit, but this in turn makes the accomplishment of landing one the height of an angler's career—even if they only ever land one.

# RED DRUM

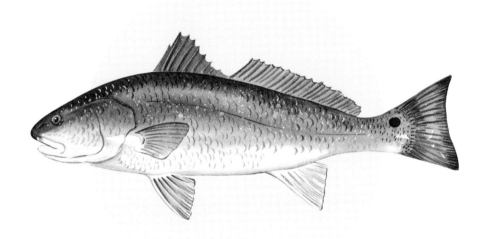

| |  | · 35 POUNDS (16 KG), OVER 45 INCHES (1.1 M) · |
|---|---|---|
| | **DIFFICULTY** | **TROPHY SIZE** |

| | |
|---|---|
| **PERFECT SPOT** | Ocracoke, United States; Mississippi Delta, United States |
| **PREFERRED HABITAT** | Small drum can be caught in virtually any inshore waters south of the Chesapeake Bay, but prefer shallow, backwater areas. Large drum are almost always found in the open ocean, except when coming inshore for spawning. Regardless of size, drum are strong swimmers who use current and structure to their advantage— optimum water temperature is 70 to 90°F (21 to 32°C). |
| **SEASON** | They can be caught year-round depending on the region; most areas are early spring through late fall. |
| **TOP TECHNIQUE** | Pieces of cut bait work for all sizes of fish, particularly larger "bull reds." For smaller fish, lures and flies of just about any variety can work; however, the gold spoon is a redfish classic that has been productive for decades. |
| **AVERAGE SIZE** | 2 to 15 pounds (0.9 to 7 kg); 15 to 35 inches (38 to 89 cm) |
| **RECORD SIZE LOCATION & DATE** | 94 pounds 2 ounces (43 kg); North Carolina, United States, 1984 |

## RED DRUM, ALSO KNOWN AS RED FISH, ARE A SCRAPPY

inshore species that are one of the absolute favorites of anglers along the Atlantic coast. They are so named for their striking rusty-red backs, and the loud drumming sound they make with their swim bladders when threatened or during spawning. Red drum are roughly tubular in shape—particularly when young—but stocky and more heavily proportioned in the first third, with a soft, broad tail. Beyond their red color, they are most well known for having a black spot at the base of the tail. This "eye spot" is an evolved feature that tricks predators into thinking the tail is the head, and when they attack, it helps the drum escape. Drum have downward facing mouths, which they use to feed off the bottom and vacuum up prey like crabs and shrimp. However, they are far from picky, and also have teeth, and will pursue and attack baitfish and other free-swimming prey. When young, red drum are often called "puppy drum," while the larger fish are called "bull reds" or simply "bulls." Red drum have an interesting growth curve, growing fast in the first 5 or so years, where they may reach upward of 30 inches (76 cm). From there, they slow down dramatically and while some fish can grow large—exceeding 70 pounds (32 kg)—some 50-year-old fish might not be much larger than 20 pounds (9 kg). This depends on a complex web of environmental factors, and fish in different regions grow at different rates.

Fishing for red drum can be split into two different categories based on the size being targeted. Puppy drum can essentially be found anywhere inshore along their home range, starting in the Gulf of Mexico and then along the Atlantic coast to the Chesapeake Bay. In addition to ocean shorelines, they invade shallow bays, marshes, estuaries, creeks, and sandy flats. They are extremely aggressive and adaptable and will chase anything they can grab—from crabs and shrimp, to fish and worms. Puppy drum will readily take any bait and they've been caught on virtually every lure out there. This is part of what makes them so popular. Like striped bass or largemouth, they can be pursued in the way the angler loves the most. In particular, sight fishing for smaller drum in the extremely skinny waters has exploded in popularity in the last few decades. Particularly in the shallow estuary and grassy regions of the Gulf of Mexico, anglers use poling skiffs to pursue these feisty fish into just inches of water, through channels and immense weedy flats. To fool these fish—whose backs and tails may be sticking out of the shallow water—they hunt them with stealth and precision casts from a distance. Seeing a "tailing" redfish turn and slurp up a fly or small, realistic-looking soft plastic can be ultra-rewarding, and the resulting drag-burning fight will bring a beaming smile to any angler's face. With high numbers of these smaller fish, anglers can experience this again and again and get repeated adrenaline hits that come with this rewarding fishing.

Hunting bulls is often much different. Bull reds are much less adaptable to salinity and temperature compared to the puppy drum, and as such are found in the deeper waters of large bays, along open ocean beaches, and farther offshore. While it's not rare for bull reds to take a jig or a lure, it's not nearly as common as with smaller fish. This is in part because as they grow large, they change behavior from chasing their food to scrounging and scavenging for weak, dying, and dead prey. This isn't to say that bulls won't attack a school of bait, or dart after a fleeing shrimp—it's just much less common. This is also why they feed more heavily in stronger currents, rougher water, bad weather, and under the cover of darkness—it increases their efficiency. Bulls also grow picky, wary, and discerning, and get much tougher to trick with lures and flies. Trophy hunting for bull reds is also much more of a game of tracking and fishing the right conditions and tides than it is with puppy drum, and an angler must be more "dialed in" to their behavior in their region. Along their entire range, trophy bull hunters focus their efforts around inlets in particular, where the large fish use the current to their advantage, gobbling up anything that gets too close—dead or alive.

To that point, bulls are much more easily caught on cut or live bait. While puppy drum are as well, it's just not as critically important. The scent of bait is key when targeting the big drum, as it draws fish from a distance and ensures the wary bull is fooled. As a result, the importance of fresh, locally caught bait is paramount when targeting bulls, with most anglers preferring one of the big three baits: shrimp, mullet, or menhaden. Bait fishing can be accomplished from both boat and shore, and a few of the most important modern saltwater bait fishing techniques have been developed through the pursuit of bull reds. And when that giant finally picks up your bait and the circle hook catches in its lip, the reward is a titanic fight with a relentless bruiser that is on par with the best of any other inshore species. The difficulty in fooling and landing a bull is the real reward, but the long, hard battle at the end is truly icing on the proverbial cake.

The most passionate redfish anglers are also naturalists, and this is independent of the size of the fish. Redfish are opportunistic and adaptable, but they are also creatures of the tides and cycles of the inshore waters. This means they follow seasonal patterns, year after year. Unlocking these patterns is part of the rewarding joy of pursuing this charismatic fish. For the most devoted, carefully tracking the moon cycles, batfish migrations, tide stages, and weather patterns becomes a critical component of the joy these fish bring. As with other species like stripers or trout, keeping a fishing journal or log that tracks all these conditions along with lures or bait that worked and the number of fish caught is helpful for continued success. This record then allows the angler ahead of time identify when conditions might be just right, instead of trying to constantly rely solely on memory. Seeing a certain pattern develop in advance and arriving with great anticipation that the fish will be there, then being totally,100 percent correct, is a feeling of accomplishment that is profound. Indeed, many anglers value this pattern recognition as much as catching the fish. Identifying those patterns over the long term can also increase fishing productivity and eliminate times or conditions that generally do not lead to any fish landed. This is why a fishing journal is so highly recommended by anglers of diverse backgrounds— not just red drum anglers. In the end, what each angler records in their journal, and whether the end result is reeling in 30 feisty puppy drum or battling a single 40-pound (18 kg) bull, simply comes down to the flavor of redfish the fisherman or -woman enjoys the most.

# ROOSTERFISH

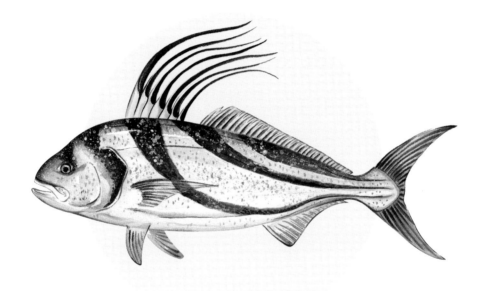

| | |
|---|---|
| **DIFFICULTY** | **· OVER 50 INCHES (1.3 M);**<br>**50 POUNDS (23 KG) ·**<br>**TROPHY SIZE** |

| | |
|---|---|
| **PERFECT SPOT** | La Paz, Baja California, Mexico; West Coast, Costa Rica |
| **PREFERRED HABITAT** | Coastal waters along Southern California, Mexico, and Central America with an optimum water temperature of 70 to 85°F (21 to 29°C). Roosterfish hunt schools of bait close to shore, around both soft and hard structure. |
| **SEASON** | Warmer months from spring through late fall. |
| **TOP TECHNIQUE** | Live or dead anchovies are the best way to guarantee a take by a rooster, but most anglers will agree catching them on topwater poppers is the most fun. |
| **AVERAGE SIZE** | 30 to 40 inches (0.8 to 1 m);<br>12 to 25 pounds (5 to 11 kg) |
| **RECORD SIZE LOCATION & DATE** | 114 pounds (52 kg);<br>Baja California, Mexico, 1960 |

# BEAUTY IS IN THE EYE OF THE BEHOLDER, AND EVERY ANGLER

that beholds the roosterfish sees the beauty. There is, quite literally, nothing like the roosterfish. "Roosters" are the only species in their genus, having been separated from similar species when it was discovered their swim bladder is connected to their ear—an adaptation that is relatively uncommon, and allows them to have excellent vibrational and hearing senses. Yet, it is their outward appearance that so spectacularly sets them apart. They are teardrop shaped, tapering from their head to highly forked tails, but thin when viewed straight on, like a mahi-mahi or crappie. Their flanks range from blue-ish gray to almost white, are brushed with iridescent greens and blues, and have 4 bold black horizontal bands, one of which runs over their eye. Their namesake comes from the dramatic 7 frills (the "rooster comb") that extend from the top of their bodies, which are extensions of the dorsal fin. This can be raised or lowered, and while the exact purpose is still being studied, there are theories it may help with everything from stability during high-speed attacks and herding prey to intimidating competitors or potential predators. Regardless, it creates a distinct, striking profile that is categorically unique.

Roosterfish are legendary, hellacious tackle busters. They are a potent mixture of fast, strong, and large, but their strange body shape and willingness to feed close to shore often catches anglers off guard and under gunned. They are just as capable of rocketing away on blistering 100 yard (91 m) runs, as they are hunkering down in the current or waves and applying crushing weight. In essence, they have all the characteristics and qualities of a pelagic species— perhaps even more wicked in attitude—yet feed in water that is only a few feet deep, tight to shore. Roosters are also boldly aggressive, intensely curious, and will give chase to anything. The hard part is getting them to hit. They are well known to be discerning, and fussy, and they turn away from a lure at the last moment, even after charging it at full speed or chasing it for long distances.

Roosterfish can be found from the southern Pacific of North America southward through Central America. They are often caught in and around the Baja of California and are very popular as a target in Costa Rica. From a boat, anglers often find them mixed in with pelagics that come in relatively close to shore chasing schools of anchovies. Boat anglers love roosters, and they provide top-level rod bending fun, on par with any of the greats. Yet, few would argue that the most passionate and dedicated rooster anglers are those who hunt them from shore. The use of the word "hunt" is intentional, because catching roosters from terra firma is akin to hunting elk or bear. There are many, many hours spent waiting in ambush in likely areas, studying the comings and goings of the tide, the structure, and the movements of bait. Anglers will cover miles and miles on foot or via a 4x4 vehicle, searching endless stretches of sandy beach and rocky outcrops. They will then set up in the most prime spot and begin the long wait, casting poppers and stick baits to an empty sea for hours, or days, hoping to intercept a single or duo of fish. The roosters can be anywhere, but often feel like they're nowhere. While double-digit days from a boat are possible, landing a couple fish in a few days of intense fishing from shore is the norm.

Then, there are the rooster fly anglers. For these anglers, an entire week with only a single viable cast at a rooster is well within the bounds of the normal, acceptable, and anticipated. The mental and physical fortitude to "live" on the beach for 12 hours a day, every day, scanning and searching, requires a deep well of dedication. Then, when a rooster pops on a school of bait, to see the fly angler sprinting down the steeply pitched sand beach towards the melee, whipping a massive fly into the wash of a giant surf, is to see a person truly possessed. Yet, even when the rooster is finally hooked, the fly fisherman or -woman acknowledges most fish will be lost, and many don't give it much thought. It is part of the rules of the game, and it makes the miraculous accomplishment of landing one a prize with few equals. And there are, in turn, few equals to anglers as uniquely dedicated as those that attempt it.

**INSHORE**

# SEA TROUT

| | · 30 INCHES (76 CM) · |
|---|---|
| **DIFFICULTY** | **TROPHY SIZE** |

| | |
|---|---|
| **PERFECT SPOT** | Corpus Cristi, Texas, United States; Tangier Island, Virginia, United States |
| **PREFERRED HABITAT** | Speckled trout, a type of sea trout, are found in a wide array of environments along their range, but they're often targeted on shallow flats with sea grass and oyster beds with an optimum water temperature of 60 to 80°F (16 to 27°C). |
| **SEASON** | Trout are caught throughout the year in their southern ranges, but follow bait schools northward in spring and summer, returning south in the fall. |
| **TOP TECHNIQUE** | Trout are easiest to catch with appropriately sized live bait and finesse soft plastics, but there is no question top water is the most fun. Try walk-the-dog style surface lures. |
| **AVERAGE SIZE** | 10 to 20 inches (24 to 51 cm) |
| **RECORD SIZE LOCATION & DATE** | 17 pounds 7 ounces (8 kg); Florida, United States, 1995 |

## SPECKLED TROUT ARE NOT THE BIGGEST OR STRONGEST GAME

fish, but they are one of the most important to the local communities along the Atlantic Coast. They are fished commercially, but the vast majority are caught by recreational anglers—and that is where their largest economic and cultural value lies. They are so plentiful and common that they are in the top 10 most caught species of fish in North America, a statistic that most anglers do not realize. Speckled trout attract a lot of anglers to coastal communities—both locally and through tourism.

Speckled trout's native range is the Gulf of Mexico and the Atlantic Coast northward to about Delaware. A fish of many nicknames—spotted trout, sea trout, specks, truite gris, spotted sea Teague, winter trout, and many others—they belong to the drum family: they're not actually trout at all. Specks are a very pretty fish, which most anglers are quick to appreciate. They are strikingly polished and brilliantly chrome along their flanks, with dark, perfectly round spots high on their body and through their tail. Along their backs they can be iridescent, with traces of blue, green, and purple. Their eyes are bright and high on their heads and their mouths are surprisingly bright yellow inside, with 2 large canine teeth in the dead-center of their top jaw. Overall, a very clean, brilliant, and flawless fish.

Specks are fast growing and short-lived and reach maturity in a single year. They spawn frequently when water temperatures are between 70 and 90°F (21 and 32°C), and they may reproduce as often as every couple of weeks. This is a relative rarity among sport fish, but it contributes to their robust population, and why they are so common. Specks can be found in a diverse array of aquatic environments, at nearly as diverse a spectrum of depths. Anglers hunt for them along open sandy beaches, in tidal creeks and rivers, and deep within estuaries, at any depth from less than 1 foot (30 cm) of water to more than 50 (15 m). Specks are schooling fish, and pack hunters, and they will pursue the bait wherever it goes—they are not sensitive or specific. However, most anglers will agree that specks are shallow-water hunters, and they are most synonymous with grass flats and oyster beds in the Gulf, Chesapeake, and similar waters.

As fun as it can be to catch speck after speck from a giant school, that is not how you catch the really special fish. Instead, trophy-sized specks are loners, or move in small packs, and they are often found in some of the shallowest, trickiest spots, where they dominate the food chain. They are infamous for sitting totally still in a "pothole"—an area of slightly deeper water, surrounded by shallow flats—waiting in ambush. Here, they are camouflaged, and they will wait for unsuspecting bait to be pushed to them by the coming and going of the tide.

Fishing the shallow grass flats of the Gulf for average-sized specks is fun, but fishing in the same areas for trophy-sized fish is a real challenge. When big specks are "laid up" shallow and solo, they are hard to spot, and as such, sight fishing is at best difficult, and most of the time simply impossible. Fan casting likely areas for trophy fish is a better method, either by shallow flats skiff, or on foot (an often-beloved method for speck anglers). But old, giant specks over 10 pounds (5 kg) are so rare, relying solely on lots of casts and luck is a fool's errand; instead, identifying the very best spots and patterns is everything. Knowing where and when they congregate and the precise times within the tide that they will feed most aggressively is more important than any number of casts, or any secret lure or bait. For this reason, while many anglers love and enjoy catching specks, trophy-focused trouters are fairly rare themselves, and supremely dedicated and secretive—and they keep their best spots to themselves.

**INSHORE**

# SHARKS

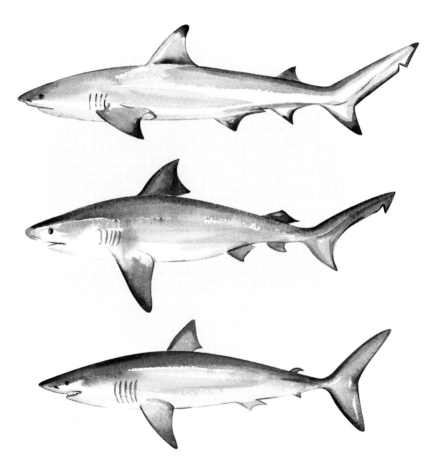

|  DIFFICULTY | · NA · TROPHY SIZE |
|---|---|
| **PERFECT SPOT** | Mako: Southern California, United States;<br>Black tip: Eastern Florida, United States;<br>Bull shark: Southeast Queensland, Australia |
| **PREFERRED HABITAT** | Sharks can be found virtually anywhere in the world's oceans, and many species come close to shore within reach of any angler. |
| **SEASON** | "Sharking" is often undertaken in summer, but sharks can be caught year-round, depending on the species and region. |
| **TOP TECHNIQUE** | A chunk of bait on a circle hook is enough to catch just about any shark—just scale the size of your hook and bait to the size of the species you're targeting. A wire leader is recommended, but not required. |
| **AVERAGE SIZE** | Not available |
| **RECORD SIZE LOCATION & DATE** | Not available |

## MANY ANGLERS DON'T REALIZE JUST HOW FUN SHARKS ARE

to catch. While it may be obvious that an 800-pound (367 kg) hammerhead or tiger shark will put up an epic fight, a 20-pound (9 kg) lemon or brown shark can be shockingly strong and fiery. In fact, many sharks—especially in warmer waters—are supremely athletic when hooked. They will take long, fast runs against heavy gear and dog anglers the entire fight, sometimes even jumping. Yet, sharks are accessible to anyone—you can catch sharks in any salt water in the world, even in the Arctic and often very close to shore without complicated gear.

For the diehard shark angler, they are the pinnacle of fishing, and adored with a deeply hallowed respect—a respect sharks do deserve, but often do not receive. Shark anglers are quick to point out that while smaller species are easy to hook, most sharks fight hard, and if you want to land ultra giants, it takes many years of honing skills: serious shark fishing is definitely not easy.

There are more than 500 species of sharks, and though many of them are small, there are an overwhelming number to catch. Each angler will have their favorites, but there are a few standouts. The first is the shortfin mako, which is one of the fastest fish in the ocean, reaching speeds of more than 40 miles per hour (64 km/h). They are ballistic fighters who grow to be 1,000 pounds (454 kg) and jump 10 or more feet (3 m) when hooked, soaring through the air in amazing displays of raw power. They are unstoppable during their first few runs even against the strongest offshore gear, and the fight with a trophy-sized mako can go on for many hours.

Blacktip sharks are a species that often gets disregarded or overlooked. They can be found all throughout the world, from right tight to the beach, all the way out into the open seas. Blacktips have a reputation for being brash and will attack anything. They are one of the only sharks that will regularly smash a popper or a plastic swimmer—you don't have to use bait to catch a blacktip.

Further, most caught are between 15 and 50 pounds (9 and 23 kg), which means they are a manageable size—catchable with typical inshore spinning gear, but still a mighty challenge. Like the mako, they are also known to burn offline, jump, and go absolutely wild once hooked.

Finally, there is the mighty bull shark. Bull sharks are amazing fish that can be found all throughout the world, in all kinds of environments. They are the only shark that can survive long periods in freshwater. They are known to travel great distances up rivers such as the Mississippi and Amazon and even into lakes and ponds. Bull sharks are supremely aggressive and will take on anything they have a chance at eating—and unlike the smaller blacktip, they get really big, reaching 500 pounds (227 kg) and 12 feet long (4 m). They are often caught close to shore in shallow waters, allowing fishermen and -women to tangle with gigantic fish without making long, fuel-intensive trips offshore. Let this be a warning however: tackling a giant bull shark is not for the meek and mild. It takes incredible stamina to fight and land a trophy bull, and the tug-of-war is a back-breaking, arm-numbing battle. Fighting the fish for too long risks injuring or killing it, so it's up to the angler to go all out.

Typical spinning inshore tackle will work for many species of sharks, all the way up to 50 or more pounds (23 kg). A steel leader is often needed, but not always, and a circle hook will keep the shark from swallowing the hook. The key to consistently landing sharks is understanding the behavior of the particular species you're targeting: when they arrive in your area, where they swim in the water column, what kind of water movement and structure they prefer, and what bait works best. Fresh bait is another critical component, and most shark diehards will tell you this is one of the most overlooked aspects of shark angling.

# SMALL TUNA

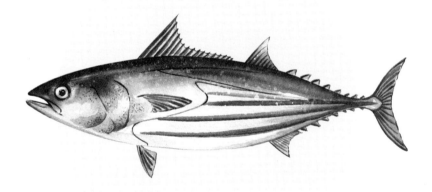

 **TO**

| DIFFICULTY | · 15 TO 40 POUNDS (7 TO 18 KG); SPECIES DEPENDENT · |
| --- | --- |
| | TROPHY SIZE |

| | |
| --- | --- |
| **PERFECT SPOT** | Outer Banks, United States; Gold Coast, Australia |
| **PREFERRED HABITAT** | Small tuna live in diverse waters throughout the world, but they generally follow bait schools. Finding the bait each species prefers is the ticket to finding these dynamic, highly migratory species. |
| **SEASON** | Highly species dependent, but most are caught in spring, summer, and fall. |
| **TOP TECHNIQUE** | Most small tuna are best caught with specialized casting lures that are small but heavy (for casting distance) and can be fished very fast—casting tins and epoxy jigs are two of the most popular. |
| **AVERAGE SIZE** | 5 to 20 pounds (2.3 to 9 kg); species dependent |
| **RECORD SIZE LOCATION & DATE** | Skipjack: 46 pounds 5 ounces (21 kg); La Gomera, Spain, 2020 Little tunny: 37 pounds (17 kg); Tarragona, Spain, 2020 Atlantic bonito: 18 pounds 4 ounces (8 kg); Azores, Portugal, 1953 |

## WHILE MOST ANGLERS PICTURE TUNA AS GIGANTIC FISH THAT

are caught in the wild, wide-open oceans of the world, there are a whole host of smaller tuna that can be caught: blackfin, black skipjack, bonito, little tunny, kawakawa, skipjack, and many others. These species range from just a couple pounds to maxing out at around 50 pounds (23 kg). All the small tuna species are extremely muscular, fast, and hunt by chasing down their prey in open water just like their bigger cousins. That means that while they're small, they pack a punch; when hooked, they rocket away with shocking speed, and are known for their fighting endurance. Since they're also schooling fish that are more manageable to land, they offer nonstop light tackle action and can be ridiculous amounts of fun for anglers of all abilities.

Most of the small tunas are also very beautiful fish. Their missile-shaped bodies are typically polished chrome with lots of iridescence, and most have some dorsal patterning with various banding and stripes on their flanks. Like all tuna, they have highly forked tails which helps with their speed. All the small tunas are migratory, and move with bait availability and water temperatures, and most of the species cover huge distances each year just like their giant cousins. The skipjack tuna is the most common encountered by anglers and are found in all the oceans of the world. Skipjack—also known as striped tuna, aku, and mushmouth—max out at around 30 pounds (14 kg) and 3 feet long (91 cm) but have one of the highest muscle densities of any animal (muscle makes up over 60 percent of their total weight). They travel in huge schools containing upward of 50,000 individuals, and they feed on anything small enough to fit into their mouths. Skipjack are powerful fish that take long runs, and since they school up, it's possible to catch more than an angler's back or arms can handle—catching dozens in a single trip can be easy.

Of all the small tunas, the little tunny is the one that inspires the most resolutely obsessed anglers. Also known as the false albacore or albies, these

5- to 20-pound (2.3 to 9 kg) tuna are found throughout the Atlantic, on both sides, from New England to Southern Brazil, and the Mediterranean to Angola. Unlike skipjack that circumnavigate the globe, albies head north along the coast in spring and then south in fall. There is much anticipation among anglers waiting for albies to arrive in their area. They are notorious for being finicky and skittish, and catching them requires delicacy and careful patterning by the angler—particularly in finding likely hot spots and understanding when certain bait is more prevalent. Unlike chasing large tuna offshore, fishing for albies can sometimes feel like fishing for fast-moving saltwater trout. Casting very small lures or flies at breaking fish or setting up in a likely spot and blind casting can be highly nuanced. Don't get the wrong impression though—albies are fast and nimble; they'll nab a lure with lightning speed and then run for the horizon. The contrast between their fussy feeding habits and their savage, lights-out fighting ability makes for an addicting combination that many anglers find utterly intoxicating.

The smallest species regularly targeted by anglers is the bonito. Bonito are not actually a single species, but instead consist of 4 different tuna in the Sandra species which are found throughout the world. They are all exceptionally small, with most fish caught well below 10 pounds (5 kg). Bonito are excellent game fish, and they are known to savagely attack small lures and flies, and even topwater poppers. When hooked, they exhibit all you would expect from a 1,000-pound (454 kg) tuna, just in a much smaller package. Like the little tunny, they also come in very close to shore and can be caught without a boat, making them a prime target of all anglers from any walk of life. Fighting giant bluefin on standup tackle can be the thrill of a lifetime, but catching bonito on light tackle while walking a beautiful sandy beach with a handful of lures can be intensely rewarding too.

# SNAPPER

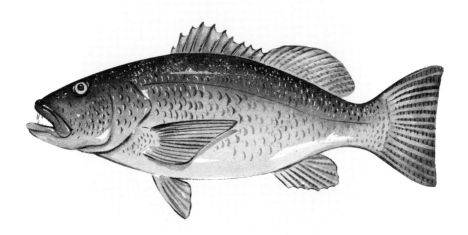

| | |
|---|---|
| **PERFECT SPOT** | Gulf of Mexico, United States; Western Atlantic, Gabon |
| **PREFERRED HABITAT** | Varies by species, but snappers generally are deep water fish (100 to 1,000 feet, or 3 to 30 m) and prefer structure such as wrecks, outcrops, and humps. |
| **SEASON** | Varies by species |
| **TOP TECHNIQUE** | Baited hooks sent down deep into the structure are the best way to catch snapper. Scale your hook and bait to the size of the fish. Many can also be caught by jigging. |
| **AVERAGE SIZE** | Varies by species, typically 1 to 10 pounds (0.5 to 5 kg) |
| **RECORD SIZE LOCATION & DATE** | Red: 50 pounds 4 ounces (23 kg); Louisiana, United States<br>Atlantic Cubera: 124 pounds 12 ounces (57 kg); Louisiana, United States<br>Squirefish: 37 pounds 14 ounces (17 kg); Mottiti Island, New Zealand |

# SNAPPERS ARE A LARGE GROUP (113 SPECIES) OF FISH

belonging to the family Lutjanidae. Virtually all snappers are marine species, and most live in deeper waters between 100 and 1,500 feet (30 to 457 m) scattered throughout the world's oceans. The species as a whole has a similar body shape—they are typically tall bodied, but thinner when viewed straight on, reminiscent in many aspects to freshwater panfish. Their tails are highly variable but are generally forked and broad. Most have smaller mouths when compared to other fish species like grouper or bass, and their eyes are positioned far forward on their heads. There are many beautiful snapper species, like the common blue stripe, sailfin, and lane snappers which are bright and colorful, covered with lots of banding and yellow coloration.

The red snapper is arguably the most popular snapper to catch, and one of the most important fish species in the Gulf of Mexico. Red snapper are prized for their delicious meat, which is served in the highest tier restaurants around the world. However, red snapper populations collapsed and are in a rebuilding phase, so the fishery is now catch and release for most of the year. The good news is the red snapper is an excellent game fish even when you can't keep any. All sizes of red snappers fight hard, but the giants are bruisers that can be tricky to land even on heavy tackle. There is a small, highly committed, and extremely ardent group of anglers that hunt leviathan reds all year long, no matter if they can harvest them or not.

Cubera snapper are the meanest, baddest snapper, and the largest by a wide margin. Some reach monstrous sizes: they can be 5 feet (1.5 m) long and exceed 100 pounds (45 kg). They are wicked looking, with huge canine teeth that are like daggers poking out of their mouths. Their broad bodies and tails are massively powerful, and fighting a giant cubera snapper is exciting, but also exhausting. Like many other fish in their family, cubera are most often caught in and around heavy structure. When hooked, these super-sized snappers dig hard for the bottom and dive directly into the thick of rock piles and wrecks. If the angler doesn't horse them out immediately, they will break even 100-pound (45 kg) leaders in a split second. Therefore, when tackling cubera, there is no room to play the fish: either you get them up and out or you lose them.

There are lots of other amazing snappers that can be caught around the globe. In the subtropical and tropical waters of the Atlantic, the yellowtail is relatively small, but can be caught in great numbers. It is exceedingly great to eat—a local favorite. In the same waters, the mutton snapper is a tough, scrappy fighter who puts up a serious battle on inshore spinning gear. In the western Pacific, the squirefish (also known as the silver sunbeam and Australasian snapper) is a big snapper with dental work that nearly rivals the cubera. This beloved fish is a heavyweight slugger, maxing out around 30 pounds (14 kg), with a penchant for breaking lines and annihilating drags.

Most snapper species are pursued with baited hooks around deep water structure. The size and type of bait is dependent entirely on the species. For example, red snapper are big: large live and dead baits such as whole pinfish or croaker are best. The same goes for cuberas, but you can go even larger with your bait. On the other end of the spectrum, for the more diminutive yellowtail, small strips of bait are fished on multiple hooks. Many anglers also will anchor up near structure and chum to call in snappers like yellowtail, vermilion, and mutton. That said, while live bait is the go-to, many snapper species can be caught on jigs and lures. Vertical jigging can be particularly exciting, but some species can even be caught on surface lures, such as poppers and sliders. The mighty cubera is one of them, and it is considered one of the highest honors in angling to land a trophy-sized cubera on a lure.

# SNOOK

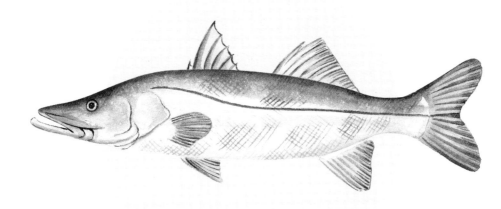

| | |
|---|---|
|  | **· COMMON SNOOK:**<br>**40 INCHES (1 M) ·** |
| DIFFICULTY | TROPHY SIZE |

| | |
|---|---|
| **PERFECT SPOT** | 10,000 Islands, United States; San Juan River, Costa Rica |
| **PREFERRED HABITAT** | Brackish and tidal waters, such as tidal creeks, rivers, canals and bays with heavy structure. Snook won't be found far from hiding places. |
| **SEASON** | Snook can be caught year-round, but their feeding behavior is heavily dependent on water temperatures staying above 70°F (21°C). |
| **TOP TECHNIQUE** | Nothing beats catching snook on top-water poppers. However, trophy anglers prefer large live baits. |
| **AVERAGE SIZE** | Common snook: 15 to 25 inches (38 to 64 cm) |
| **RECORD SIZE LOCATION & DATE** | Common snook: 53 pounds 10 ounces (24 kg); Parismina River, Costa Rica 1978 |

# THE SNOOK ARE A HANDSOME, ATLANTIC INSHORE FISH, WITH

polished silver sides, a single dramatic black stripe that runs the length of their body, and pale-yellow fins that match the coloration along their backs. Their body is typically proportioned, but they have a heavily sloped and broad head that ends in a mouth that has a small underbite when closed. Their eyes are ringed with a slim, gold border and are situated high on the sides of their head.

Several snook species can be caught, and they are all found from approximately the southern part of Georgia through the Caribbean to Brazil, including throughout much of the Gulf of Mexico. The common snook is the species most likely to be encountered and they are completely adaptable in tolerating any salinity level. You can fish for them in the wide-open ocean on reefs and deeper structure, but also in freshwater ponds, swamps, and canals. They regularly switch back and forth as conditions in one type of water become more favorable over the other. As long as the water is clean, has plenty of food, and primarily stays above 60°F (16°C)—even though they prefer 70 to 80°F (21 to 27°C)—snook will make it their home regardless if it's fresh or salt. However, they thrive in and around brackish waters where they can dominate the top of the food chain and hunt their preferred food: baitfish.

Snook are "trolls under the bridge"—patient ambushers, waiting until unsuspecting bait swims by, and then darting out in a lightning fast, savage, "all-or-nothing" attack. They are very structure-oriented fish, rarely chasing their prey any distance, and they prefer cover over their heads. For this reason, they love hiding under docks, up inside mangrove roots, deep within wrecks, and tucked into floating aquatic vegetation. Snook also associate with shadow lines, where they will lay in the dark and use it to surprise prey that comes too close. While it isn't essential, they also like some water movement or current that will carry food their way.

The nature of a snook to favor certain bits of structure and remain in the same place means anglers can find predictable "snook spots." Snook are known for feeding heaviest during certain windows of time and environmental conditions. Since they stay put and react routinely to specific conditions, anglers can find very robust patterns as to when and where snook are most likely to feed. Identifying what tide, wind, and weather is best for each spot is a significant undertaking that takes years to lock down, but once you have a solid pattern, it can be incredibly rewarding. This, in combination with the snook's size, strength, and its ability to live anywhere, fuels an obsession that makes it the favorite of many hardcore local and traveling anglers.

The snook is a bulldog, and when hooked, it does its best to remain at home base. This means the beginning of a battle with a snook—especially a large one—must be savage. Moving them away from that structure as quickly as possible is essential, because they will do their best to break you off on anything and everything. It's a tense few moments, yanking a big, fired-up snook out of a mangrove, or steering them away from pilings. But even after you tow them out, they are powerful and will take long runs, sometimes jumping, and often shaking their head at the surface in an effort to throw the hook.

Snook are willing to hit a variety of baits, lures, and flies. Trophy fishermen and -women generally sling giant live baits—like adult mullet and pinfish—in large tidal rivers and bays, and around inlets and outflows. Those less concerned about size and more about quantity will find that soft- and hard-plastic lures work well in all waters, especially around mangroves and smaller waterways. Catching fish on top-water lures is highly addictive, as the explosions a snook makes when it commits to something on the surface is violent, savage, and will get any angler's heart pounding. Fly fishing for these fish is popular and continues to get more so, and sight casting to a 30-plus-inch (76 cm) snook is a bucket list challenge.

# STRIPED BASS

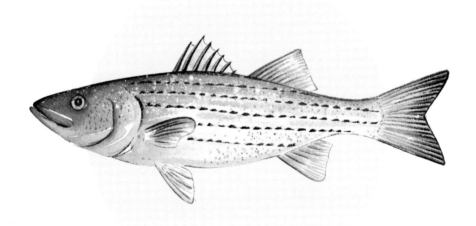

| | |
|---|---|
|  | **· 35 POUNDS (16 KG);**<br>**OVER 45 INCHES (1.1 M) ·** |
| DIFFICULTY | TROPHY SIZE |

| | |
|---|---|
| **PERFECT SPOT** | Montauk Point, Montauk, NY, United States;<br>Casco Bay, United States |
| **PREFERRED HABITAT** | Any inshore waters along their range can hold stripers with an optimum water temperature of 50 to 75°F (10 to 24°C). However, they are most often found near rocky shorelines, along inshore rips, and in inlets, outflows, and estuaries. |
| **SEASON** | Stripers can be caught all year depending on the region and in most areas from spring through late fall. |
| **TOP TECHNIQUE** | During the day, topwater walk-the-dog lures or sight fishing with a fly rod can't be beat, but at night, plastic minnow swimmers or live eels rule. |
| **AVERAGE SIZE** | 3 to 20 pounds (1.4 to 9 kg);<br>20 to 35 inches (51 to 89 cm) |
| **RECORD SIZE LOCATION & DATE** | 81 pounds 14 ounces (37 kg), 54 inches (1.4 m);<br>Connecticut, United States, 2011 |

## STRIPED BASS ARE AN INSTANTLY RECOGNIZABLE FISH. THEY

are so named for the 7 jet-black stripes that run down their pearly, softly scaled flanks. They're mostly monochrome, but in the warm glow of a rising sun, a sheen of iridescent blues, greens, and copper will appear along their back and sides. A rugged, tough inshore fish, the "striper" is tubular and muscular from end to end. They have bucket-shaped mouths, and, besides the stripes, are best known for their broad "broom shaped" tails, which hint at both their strength and some of their most exceptional traits.

The hardy, adaptable nature of stripers allows them to thrive in an astoundingly diverse array of marine environments. They can be found in every nook and cranny along their native range, from tiny tidal creeks to inshore boulder fields to offshore canyons. This ability to flourish just about anywhere is a perfect match for their appetite: they'll eat virtually anything. They are opportunists and will attack whatever comes too close or they think they can chase down—from shrimp, worms, and squid to 10-pound (5 kg) blue fish or adult lobsters, and even other smaller stripers.

One of the most incredible attributes of the striper is their epic biannual migration. Between 75 and 90 percent of the entire population spawns in the Chesapeake Bay in North America, with much of the population overwintering there. Once spawning in the Chesapeake Bay is complete in the spring, millions of fish will gradually work their way north from Virginia to Maine. The majority of the best striper fishing is seasonal—they move into an area in spring as they migrate, stay some period of time, and then leave again in the fall. Depending on where it is along the coast, they may stay as little as a few weeks or as long as 5 months before moving again. That characteristic builds both intense anticipation waiting for stripers to arrive in the spring, and a sense of urgency to get out and fish for them when they are in the area. Then, as the weather cools in early fall, the stripers turn around again and head south—this is when striper fever really takes hold.

In autumn, a mix of variables come together to create intense, awe-inspiring striper fishing. Stripers need to put on weight to survive the cold, dark days to come, and become aggressive and emboldened. They school up and move in immense groups. Their survival-fueled fall appetite is ratcheted up further by pack induced competition, making them extra belligerent and savage. At the same time, young of the year baitfish (born in the spring) are leaving their nursery grounds in estuaries and rivers and heading out to sea. The result is a powder keg, which explodes into feeding frenzies up and down the coast, very close to shore. This is a visual spectacle that is unparalleled, with gigantic schools of baitfish fleeing in a panic while flocks of seabirds dive relentlessly on the hapless prey and thousands of stripers attack from below. The fishing can be equally outrageous to match—for hours, or even days.

While it can be some of the most exciting fishing of the season, in truth most of the striper season is not made up of these legendary events. Instead, anglers target stripers primarily by focusing on tidal currents and structure (such as boulder fields, sand bars, and inlets). Stripers are the champions of the current, and it draws them like a magnet. They use those big broom tails to overpower any bait in current, and nothing can escape a big, persistent striper. For this reason, the best fishing is associated with new and full moons, when the tidal currents are strongest, and during storm fronts when waves and undertow are most intense. No tidal rip or storm surge is too much for these relentless predators, and when a jumbo striper turns on prey in fast-moving water, nothing escapes. The other key to catching stripers—especially trophy-sized ones—is focusing effort around low-light periods (dawn, dusk, and inclement weather) and after dark. While they can feed aggressively during the day, they are primarily nocturnal hunters and many top-level striper anglers will only fish at night. This presents another level of difficulty and excitement to striper fishing and is part of their charm. If you want the highest probability of catching a "cow," then fishing after dark in inclement weather will increase your chances considerably.

The striped bass has also been introduced to several other places in the world. In California, there is a self-sustaining population that breeds in the estuaries and rivers leading into the Pacific. This entire population was transported from the East Coast via train and railway car in the 1800s, and now swims in the tidal waters of the Pacific Ocean. It is a controversial fishery, as the striper has been implicated in the continued demise of Pacific salmon species, but for now, the population continues to thrive. There are also several distinct populations in Canada that no longer interact with the main, native population of stripers in the Northeast. The largest concentration is found around the Gaspe Peninsula, and after a total population collapse, it has soared in number in recent years. Canadian anglers are once again discovering the majesty and joy of fishing for stripers in waters they were once native to. Finally, there are also landlocked, freshwater stripers that have been stocked in lakes throughout the country—along both coasts and throughout the interior—as well as several different hybrid species that have arisen from cross breeding with other species. These freshwater populations are extremely popular, as those stripers can still reach weights in excess of 40 pounds (18 kg) and offer another highlight of the adaptability of the species.

Stripers can be caught using an astounding number of techniques and tactics. Anglers pursue stripers in culturally distinct ways dependent on where they are along the coast, the type of structure they fish, the time of year, and their independent personalities. Essentially, the striper can be anything you want it to be. Whether caught with a fly rod and a flats skiff, a center console and live eels, a kayak and a top-water popper, or a pair of waders and a lead jig, the opportunities to pursue stripers in exactly the way you want is one of the incredibly special things about these beloved fish. There is no "best way," instead, it's as much about the angler's preference as anything else. That being said, using custom wood lures is a relatively unique attribute of the striper world. Craftsmen carve amazingly lifelike bait fish replicas from blocks of wood, laboring tirelessly to create specialized lures that perform exactly the way they want for the specific spots and scenarios they fish.

While most stripers are caught from a boat, there is a large contingent of hardened anglers who pursue the fish only from shore. For the "surfcaster" there is no fish like the striper: they get big, they come in close, and they recklessly chase lures. Surfcasters highly prefer fishing at night and in rugged, blustery conditions when the best fishing occurs tight to shore. Taking on the challenge of the weather and waves can be just as exciting as catching the fish. Many striper anglers, especially surfcasters, tend to be somewhat secretive—hiding their secret spots and lures from other anglers. Fishing alone is common, and surfcasters can get particularly obsessive over the hunt for their beloved striper. There are many fanatical fishermen and -women across different species of fish, and striper boat anglers can be very devoted, analytical, and talented. However, the most infatuated surfcasters are some of the most obsessed anglers in the world—or addicted, depending on your perspective.

# TARPON

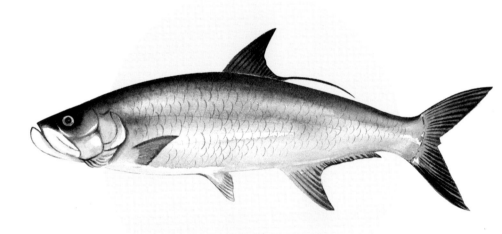

| | · 150 POUNDS (68 KG) · |
|---|---|
| **DIFFICULTY** | **TROPHY SIZE** |

| | |
|---|---|
| **PERFECT SPOT** | Islamorada, United States; Manzanillo, Costa Rica |
| **PREFERRED HABITAT** | Tarpon can be found in the waters of the Atlantic, from roughly Virginia through South America, as well as along the African coastline. Adults are primarily caught in shallow inshore waters with current, but juveniles are more often found in brackish waters. Tarpon are warm water fish; they are caught when the water is between 75 and 90°F (24 to 32°C). |
| **SEASON** | March through June and September through October |
| **TOP TECHNIQUE** | The easiest way to fool a tarpon is with live bait. However, many techniques have been employed to catch tarpon with artificials, including jigs and soft plastics. While it has become more common, landing a tarpon on the fly remains one of the top achievements within the sport worldwide. |
| **AVERAGE SIZE** | 20 to 70 pounds (9 to 32 kg) |
| **RECORD SIZE LOCATION & DATE** | 286 pounds 9 ounces (130 kg); Rubane, Guinea-Bissau, 2003 |

## TARPON ARE A TOP CONTENDER FOR THE GREATEST INSHORE

game fish. Tarpon combine an amalgamation of characteristics that create an adversary which is unparalleled, even compared to pelagics, while simultaneously being accessible in a way that exotic offshore species are not. In turn, they have been pursued with a fervent lust by an astounding percentage of the best anglers of multiple generations; some of the most skilled and innovative anglers in history have been tarpon fanatics. Many lives have been fulfilled fishing for the "silver king," and there is something about the pursuit of this magnanimous fish that grabs ahold of your heart and soul and never lets go. Throughout history, professional athletes, celebrities, musicians, authors, and even presidents have been held in rapture by tarpon.

Tarpon are alien-looking fish. They are elongated, and their bodies are tall, but compressed so they appear thin straight on. Covering their flanks are huge, highly polished scales that both look and act like plates of armor. A black or dark green back extends to their deeply forked tail, but their flanks are as reflective as a mirror (hence the nickname "silver king"). This attribute, along with the shape of their body, gives them the appearance of a blade of steel, an apt metaphor for their fighting prowess and overall rugged nature. Their gill plates are large and rock hard, and their upturned mouths are massive and bucket shaped. They are a tough opportunistic fish that will eat anything, live long (over 50 years), and easily eclipse 150 pounds (68 kg). They can also thrive in a huge spectrum of environments on both coasts of the Atlantic, from open ocean reefs to inshore sand flats, and mangrove backwaters.

The scientific name for tarpon—*Megalops*—is a nod to their exceptionally large eyes. The size of their eyes underlies their astounding vision, which is unique when compared to any other creature in the animal kingdom. Tarpon have very good night vision, with lots of rod cells and a highly-reflective tapetum lucidum, which is a coating on the back of the eye that helps them capture more light. This helps them feed under low-light conditions, and primarily after dark. But they can also see very well during the day, and it was recently discovered that they also have 5 different kinds of cone cells—this is exceptional for any fish. This means that they are able to detect 100 million different shades of color—this vastly exceeds a human's already exceptional ability to see about a million, and most animals' ability to see far, far less. Together with their amazing night vision and ability to track fast-moving prey, it's no wonder tarpon are so notorious for inspecting, and then rejecting, even the most realistic lure or fly.

Unbeknownst to most anglers, the insatiable drive to catch tarpon is generally accepted as what was responsible for launching the entire world of big-game sport fishing. For centuries, a trophy-sized tarpon was considered uncatchable—and they were actively avoided—until the first was landed on a bamboo rod in 1885. That 93-pound (42 kg) fish started a revolution. Anglers flocked to Southwest Florida amid the rumors, and more and more tarpon were landed through the turn of the twentieth century. Then, rod and reel technology advanced rapidly in response to the new demands of saltwater sportfishing—much spurred by tarpon—and other formerly uncatchable species started being landed. Tarpon angling then exploded in popularity in the 1940s and '50s when books, articles, and photos of tarpon started to circulate worldwide, and this put tarpon on a sanctified pedestal—where they still remain today.

The reason tarpon are so revered is multifaceted, but a major component is how devilishly hard they are to land. Tarpon are sly and fickle, and many anglers will even go so far as to say they're "moody." Particularly during the day in shallow water, tarpon are known to ignore even the best placed live baits, lures, and flies. Even when they follow or give chase, they are notorious for then suddenly turning off at the last moment and snubbing the angler's best attempt.

It can be infuriating, even for the most even-keeled anglers, and what worked yesterday in landing double-digit numbers (a rare feat), might not work again for months—or ever again. While it's a stretch to call any fish smart, tarpon are certainly supremely adept at detecting if something is safe to eat or not, and subject to wildly divergent feeding behaviors. Therefore, while the ultimate goal is landing the fish, many anglers consider it a win just to see a tarpon eat their lure or fly, and have it jump after being hooked.

That said, getting a tarpon to eat is the easy part: fighting them is the larger hurdle. Tarpon are a frightening combination of big, fast, strong, and determined. When hooked they take explosive, blistering runs, and are adept at using their blade-like bodies and large tails to dive hard and produce massive pressure even on heavy tackle. Tarpon are adapted to live in hot, poorly oxygenated waters, so they fatigue very slowly and have extreme levels of endurance. They also have a secret weapon: they can breathe air, gulping it at the surface and storing it in their swim bladder for use during the fight, giving them extra bursts of power and endurance.

Then, there is the profundity of the tarpon's jump. The visage of a tarpon taking flight can change an angler; there is nothing quite like it. The majesty and violence of it is a metaphor for the power of the sea, the raw embodiment of the natural world. It cannot be overstated how dramatic their jump is, as they flail, cartwheel, and tail-walk over and over, all at lightning speed, in an attempt to free themselves from the line. When a tarpon takes flight, it swings its head so hard and fast side to side, that its steely, armor-like gill plates create wicked leverage that can dislodge even the sharpest, best-placed hook. It has been said that the jump of an angler's first big tarpon may be the single most transformative moment in their lifetime of angling—it is truly that transformative of a sight. No one ever gets over the spectacle of it. The only hope is to "bow to the cow;" a technique developed by tarpon anglers in which

the angler drops the rod tip and points it at the tarpon as it jumps, creating a bit of slack so the fish can't use the force of the line to help yank the hook. Unlike many other species, tarpon don't just jump at the beginning of the fight either, but instead are known to "go off" and take flight at any moment.

The sheer athleticism and power of the jump is enough to break heavy line, but it also has another purpose. It takes advantage of yet another eminently challenging characteristic of the silver king: its concrete-hard jaw. Their huge mouth is all bone and cartilage, with few soft fleshy parts like other fish species. Their hard mouths evolved to protect them from the spines of fish and hard shells of crustaceans. This means getting a hook to penetrate takes a tremendous amount of force, while at the same time having little flesh for the hook to catch in. Getting a good hookset comes down to savagely repeated sets by the angler, with the best, sharpest hooks they can find, and a good dose of luck.

All these factors come together to create a supremely unique and challenging game fish. Yet, this same difficult nature instills unrivaled dedication and obsession, too. The best, most dedicated tarpon anglers are legendary for their angling talents—from their fishing fighting and casting abilities to their tackle innovations, to their understanding of the natural world, to their observant and meticulous nature. Truly, tarpon diehards—the ones who rearrange their entire lives around the tarpon season—have few equals in all the world of fishing. The passion anglers have for tarpon goes to their very bones, deep into their soul, and it can feel like divine purpose chasing these astounding fish.

# BLACK AND BLUE MARLIN

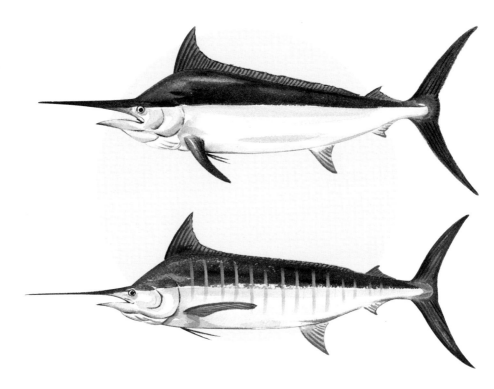

| | AT LEAST 700 POUNDS (318 KG); REGION SPECIFIC · |
|---|---|
| **DIFFICULTY** | **TROPHY SIZE** |

| | |
|---|---|
| **PERFECT SPOT** | Cape Verde Islands, Republic of Cabo Verde; Hawaii Islands, United States |
| **PREFERRED HABITAT** | Marlin are pelagic fish that are always on the move. They hunt at a wide spectrum of depths, following ocean currents and bait schools. They have a very wide preferred temperature range but mostly 70 to 90°F (21 to 32°C). Finding marlin can be complicated and takes years of experience; it's best to learn from an experienced captain. |
| **SEASON** | Marlin are caught year-round as they move through the world's oceans. |
| **TOP TECHNIQUE** | Trolling large, multi-component lures (like spreader bars and dredge lures) are the most popular method for attracting marlin. Once close to the boat, tossing them a huge live bait is the go-to for ensuring a hookup. Then, hold on for the fight of your life. |
| **AVERAGE SIZE** | 200 to 500 pounds (91 to 227 kg) |
| **RECORD SIZE LOCATION & DATE** | Blue marlin: 1,402 pounds 2 ounces (636 kg); Vitoria, Brazil, 1992<br>Black marlin: 1,560 pounds (708 kg); Cabo Blanco, Peru, 1953 |

## WHILE THIS BOOK WAS NEVER INTENDED TO RANK SPECIES OF

sportfish, it's hard to deny that the blue marlin and black marlin are at number one. If you know nothing about these fish, then imagine all this: First, marlin can reach upward of 14 feet (4 m) long and some are rumored to weigh nearly a ton. Second, they live in the last totally wild frontier on Earth, the wide-open seas. In these wild waters, they travel thousands of miles a year, and at times more than 100 miles (1,609 m) in a single day, never stopping for their entire lives. There are no limits to where you can find them in the water column either—they might be feeding on the surface or over 2,000 feet (610 m) deep. Finally, they are ruthless and relentless predators, and since they get so huge, they eat other large, powerful gamefish like 50-pound (23 kg) tuna. And to subdue their super-sized prey, they use blistering speed to catch it and then a massive, baseball-bat-thick bill to club, stun, and injure it before swallowing it whole. It's no wonder then that they are considered the most intimidating fish to pursue and require a resolute commitment on several levels by any angler brave enough to take them on.

There are 11 species of marlin, all of which are formidable and difficult fish to catch. That said, the blue marlin and black marlin are by far the largest. Both have long, sword-like bills and heavy, deeply shouldered bodies with massive, forked tails. The black marlin, as its name implies, is darker in coloration, and its dorsal fin is huge and not retractable, while the blue marlin is more silver, with a striking dark blue stripe that runs the length of its body, and it can retract its large dorsal fin. The black marlin is also stockier, with heavier shoulders and a deeper body, whereas the blue marlin is leaner and longer.

A marlin's entire survival is predicated on their immense strength, speed, and stamina, and they use this power against anglers. A hooked marlin is a spectacle of chaos like no other. Blue marlin in particular will rocket to 50 miles an hour (80 km/h) in seconds and run for hundreds of yards against a 100-pound (45 kg) test line. Both species jump entirely out of the water, upward of 30 or more times, and skim along the surface like a skipping stone—over 1,000 pounds (454 kg) of flying, raging, fury! Yet, the fight turns particularly brutal when they decide to finally veer down, and dive into the dark abyss. At this point they can use endurance to break the will of the angler over the course of long, tiring hours—they can even take on a whole team of anglers, and still defeat them all. There is no doubt: The marlin's combined ability to run, jump, and dive has no parallel in the angling world. Most anglers will agree that the blue marlin is the better fighter of the two behemoths, as they jump more and are just a bit more unruly, going deeper, and making more changes in depth. However, this is far from a consensus, as blacks will also go berserk, and sometimes have more endurance, though they don't generally dive as deep. It really comes down to the individual nature of every single fish hooked, and most anglers can recount differences between individuals easily. It's hard to forget any fight with a marlin!

Due to the immensity of their power and outrageous fighting ability, landing a marlin successfully is not something that comes naturally. Only through experience can an angler gain the confidence and composure to land a really big marlin. Though it's often a painful process, this often means losing a lot of fish before finally landing one. When hunting trophies of other species, most anglers downplay the necessity of failure. Making mistakes, and then learning from them, gives the angler the knowledge of what to do when things start to go wrong—or when to make the most of any advantages the fish gives them. This is true of any trophy fish of freshwater or saltwater but is typified by the almighty marlin. You must fail, and fail a lot, before you will ever succeed.

This raises an important point: while most fish in these pages can be pursued by casual anglers, this is not true of the indomitable marlin. While fighting and landing the fish is difficult, the barriers to getting started are even higher; fishing for marlin requires very expensive equipment and dedicated offshore vessels, and the fuel bill alone can be astronomical. There is also the investment of hundreds (or, more typically, thousands) of hours on the water that is required just to begin to find marlin, let alone consistently hook them. It's a long, hard grind with a steep learning curve, and the rate of failure is staggering. There are very few casual marlin captains partly because of this—it requires an all-in commitment, an entire lifestyle dedication. As such, the most ferociously passionate anglers that hunt marlin with fervor do so for more than just fun, happiness, or joy—it's a pursuit that feels like a sanctified purpose. Marlin are a species that consumes the most obsessed; they feel born to pursue marlin. It's as if the rest of the angling world is colored in gray tones, and the marlin is the only species with any color. For those that take it to the ultimate level, fishing for marlin is not a pastime; it is their whole life. True, this is partly because marlin require so much time and dedication just to catch with any consistency, but it's so much more than that. The sheer power and majesty of these wild animals is an incarnation of the open blue waters themselves. To overcome and defeat one is to exert some control over one of the mightiest living forces on this planet—and that is a feeling that is unmatched by any other species.

In large part because it is so very difficult and exclusive, marlin fishing can also be highly competitive. Tournaments are some of the most extravagant events in the angling world, and there can be millions of dollars of payouts—often for a single fish—mostly funded by gambling and betting on captains and their crew. This is a long-standing part of the culture, and the stakes are as high as any angler can imagine. Boats will come from around the world to compete in the most well-known tournaments, because they're legendary for cementing captains and crews in the annals of angling history. Winning a storied tournament like the Bisbee's Black and Blue or the White Marlin Open is like winning the Super Bowl or the World Cup.

There are many other amazing things that are unique to marlin, but it would be a disservice to not specifically mention the incredible lures used to pursue them. With so much area to cover, anything that can draw a marlin's attention from a far distance is invaluable. One way this is done is by using complicated lure systems that mimic whole schools of bait. These systems are made up of many individual lures—from a half-dozen to several dozen—all connected together with thin metal arms and cables. There are many different designs, but most look like a chandelier being dragged through the water. The surprising thing is, most have no hooks. The huge multi-faceted lure is just designed to make a ton of noise and draw the fish's attention—not hook it. Once the marlin is chasing, the anglers will employ a "bait and switch." They will pull that bait-school-mimicking lure closer and closer to the boat, then yank it out of the water and cast out a big, tantalizing bait (often a live 10- to 15-pound, or 5- to 7-kg, tuna), this is called "the pitch." The marlin is in full attack mode and sees the easy meal and pounces on it—and then the angler is in for the fight of their lives.

# BLUEFIN TUNA

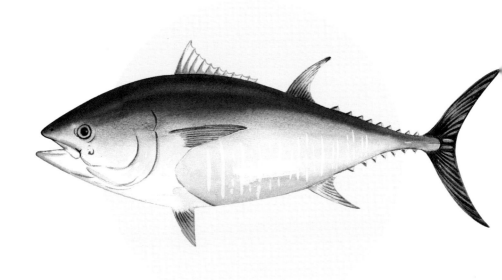

| DIFFICULTY | · 200 TO 1,000 POUNDS (91 TO 454 KG);<br>SPECIES AND REGION SPECIFIC ·<br>TROPHY SIZE |
|---|---|
| **PERFECT SPOT** | Prince Edward Island, Canada;<br>San Diego, California, United States |
| **PREFERRED HABITAT** | Bluefin are found throughout the world's oceans in temperate and colder waters. They mostly feed in the upper part of the water column but can be caught anywhere from 1,000 feet (305 m) down to right on the surface. They follow bait schools, which vary by location. |
| **SEASON** | Bluefin are caught throughout the year in different parts of the world's oceans. |
| **TOP TECHNIQUE** | If you are looking to catch a trophy fish, chunks of bait or live bait is the best bet in most cases. However, the thrill of catching bluefin on topwater poppers is hard to beat. |
| **AVERAGE SIZE** | 50 to 500 pounds (23 to 227 kg); species and region specific |
| **RECORD SIZE LOCATION & DATE** | Atlantic bluefin: 1,496 pounds (679 kg);<br>Nova Scotia, Canada, 1979 |

# IN ANY DISCUSSION OF THE HARDEST-FIGHTING FISH, THE

bluefin tuna will always rise to the top echelon. They are likely the only fish in this book to challenge the mighty marlin and swordfish, in terms of brute strength and unending stamina. While marlin are known to be chaotic and unpredictable, jumping and running like a rodeo bull, tuna are more like a rocket ship of straight-line power. They run fast and hard, and dive deep, and when (or if) they tire, they lean broadside and fight the angler with a seemingly bottomless well of devastating pull. It is debated hotly in the fishing world which fish is the hardest fighting, but the bluefin is likely the winner. Battles with 1,000-pound (454 kg) fish can take hours, even with a whole team taking turns.

Bluefin can be found throughout the world as 3 different species, which all make remarkable migrations every year. The pacific bluefin (*Thunnus orientalis*) spawn in the waters around Japan but migrate to California and New Zealand to feed and mature. The Atlantic bluefin (*Thunnus thynnusis*), is split into two distinct subpopulations. Both spend most of their time growing and maturing off the northeast Atlantic coast of the United States, but one population spawns in the Gulf of Mexico, and the other in the Mediterranean Sea. The southern bluefin (*Thunnus maccoyii*) lives throughout the Southern Hemisphere oceans, but spawns in the Indian Ocean off the northwest corner of Australia. As adults, they roam the open oceans of the world, sometimes coming close to shore, but mostly staying in deep waters and always on the move as they follow schools of bait. They feed near the surface often, but also are very comfortable diving down to 1,000 feet (305 m) if there are feeding opportunities that demand it. In essence, bluefin go anywhere their food goes, virtually limitless and boundless, and have been caught in a very wide spectrum of environments and water temperatures, from Northern Canada to the tropics of Australia and virtually everywhere in between.

All three bluefin species are similar in build and coloration. They are all rhomboid in body shape, round and rotund like a diamond with curved edges, similar to a giant football. They are supremely muscular, with very long, but relatively thin, forked tails. Unlike other fish, their bodies stay rigid while swimming, with the tail being the only part that moves back and forth. They are dark blue along their backs, silvery gray with an iridescent sheen on their flanks, with yellow dorsal fins and caudal finlets; finlets look like small yellow cones that run between their dorsal fin and tail. While the Southern and Pacific species are 1,000- and 500-pounds (454 and 227 kg), respectively, the Atlantic is the mightiest of the group, and one of the largest fish in the ocean. While the world record is nearly 1,500 pounds (680 kg), scientists and anglers speculate that they actually can get much bigger—potentially over 2,000 pounds (907 kg). Sadly, the number of really big tuna has plummeted due to overfishing, primarily due to the demand for sushi, and most fish caught now are well under 1,000 pounds (454 kg).

It's not just the fact they can reach a ton that makes them mighty. Even when they're babies—just 20 or 30 pounds (9 to 14 kg)—they are unnaturally strong, packing a punch that is far superior to other fish of similar size. This is partly because all tuna maintain a warm body temperature, as much as a whopping 10 to 15°F (6 to 9°C) warmer than the surrounding waters. They aren't warm blooded like mammals, but they capture energy generated from their muscles with a countercurrent blood exchange that prevents heat from dissipating to the environment. This keeps their muscles warm and their metabolisms very high and plays a role in their ability to swim at speeds in excess of 40 miles per hour (1.6 km/h). It also provides them with excellent vision, as they use the warmth to power their giant eyes, visual systems, and brains, even when diving deep into cold waters.

Fighting a big bluefin is violent. They are so strong that, even after an angler sets up on them with a hookset and engages the drag, the fish sometimes don't even realize they're hooked. When they do, the amount of power they produce is absurd. It can be intimidating to an angler with no experience with these behemoths, and the adrenaline that comes with doing battle with a giant tuna can be overwhelming—it can also be life changing. For the bluefin specialist, once they first get a taste of that raw, unbridled power, all other fish cease to matter. The most hardcore tuna anglers spend all year waiting for the fish to migrate to their area—planning, scheming, and preparing all winter—and then fish like men and women possessed. They spend 16 hours on the water each day, for weeks on end, having saved every vacation and sick day for those trips. Some anglers even make forays to the offshore canyons that last multiple days and nights on larger vessels.

Bluefin tuna are opportunistic fish. They eat lots of different open ocean baits, from 10 pound (5 kg) bluefish to 3-inch-long (7.5 cm) sand eels. Their diverse diet means tuna can be caught in all sorts of different ways. It partly comes down to the size of the tuna being targeted, partly where they're feeding in the water column, and partly where in the world they're being pursued. That being said, you're most likely to hear captains referring to 5 different methods for fishing for tuna: live lining, jigging, trolling, chunking, or popping. Jigging and trolling are both very effective methods, but if you're looking for engagement, there is no question that for fish under 500 pounds (227 kg), there is no greater thrill than throwing topwater poppers into schools of raging bluefin. When tuna are thrashing bait on the surface, and spraying it in the air in a full feeding frenzy, it's mayhem. The fish often come fully out of the water as they cut through schools of baitfish, with birds circling and diving from above, and very often whales also feeding right up close to the boat. These charged-up fish will detonate on a popper thrown into the melee—setting the hook and feeling the fish take off is near the pinnacle of adrenaline-inducing angling. It's also a very chaotic type of fishing, where anglers give chase at full speed in their vessels as schools pop up and then cast at fish going berserk, repeating the process until they are hooked up.

At the same time, fighting a giant 1,000-pound (454 kg) tuna on the spinning gear used for casting poppers, or even medium conventional tackle used for jigging, is virtually impossible with the current tackle technology. Most giants are taken on ultra heavy conventional gear by either trolling or using live or dead baits. Even against the strongest, most ludicrous gear—like reels that hold 1,000 yards (914 m) of 130-pound (59 kg) monofilament—bluefin still often defeat anglers. In fact, most tuna that are hooked by anglers are lost at some point during the fight, regardless of size. Whether they're 200 or 2,000 pounds (91 or 907 kg), they are simply so fast, and can change direction so quickly, they create immense instantaneous force to the line, hook, and rod. It's a lot of shock that must be overcome by the tackle and the angler, and the tiniest mistake or weakness often leads to a lost fish. Similar to fishing for the other greats—like marlin, carp, or tarpon—losing bluefin during the fight is just something that must be accepted, as it's simply part of taking on such a monumental challenge. That's just a really tough fact to remember when you lose the fish boatside after a 6-hour battle!

# GREATER
# AMBERJACK

**DIFFICULTY**

**· 75 POUNDS (34 KG) ·**

**TROPHY SIZE**

| | |
|---|---|
| **PERFECT SPOT** | Islamorada, United States; Iki Island, Japan |
| **PREFERRED HABITAT** | Amberjack are found throughout the world's warmer waters with optimal temperatures between 65 and 70°F (18 and 21°C) and at moderate depths of 50 to 500 feet (15 to 152 m). They are only found in heavy structure, such as reefs, wrecks, oil rigs, and platforms. |
| **SEASON** | Seasonal in some subtropical and temperate waters but can be caught year-round in many parts of the world. |
| **TOP TECHNIQUE** | Dropping large baits on very heavy gear directly into structure is the most popular method, but jigging for these fish with bucktail and metal jigs is effective and extremely fun. |
| **AVERAGE SIZE** | 20 to 50 pounds (9 to 23 kg) |
| **RECORD SIZE LOCATION & DATE** | 163 pounds 2 ounces (74 kg); Zenisu, Tokyo, Japan, 2015 |

# THE GREATER AMBERJACK, TYPICALLY JUST CALLED

"amberjack," is the largest species in the jack and pompano family. These heavily bodied fish are a slightly elongated football shape with the common forked tail of the family. Amberjacks vary in coloration throughout the world, but they are plainly shaded, primarily all silver sided with white bellies, with a dark dorsal side, a subtle yellow stripe on their flank, and a dark band over their eye. What they lack in appearance, they make up for in size. While most amberjack landed by anglers are around 50 pounds (23 kg), there are plenty caught weighing over 100 pounds (4 kg) and in excess of 5 feet long (1.5 m), with rumors of 200-pound (91 kg) fish circulating regularly in the angling world. These are exceptionally big, heavy, monstrous jacks.

Amberjacks have one of the best nicknames of any fish: "reef donkeys." The name comes from both their propensity to hang around heavy structure, and their stubbornness to leave it when hooked. However, that simple description does both characteristics very little justice. Amberjacks are supremely structure-oriented fish. The young are pelagic, but once they reach catchable size, they move toward the bottom and stick tight to structure like they are tethered to it—it's essentially unheard of to catch them in open water. Adults are found all over the world where there is expansive hard structure, such as giant reefs, large shipwrecks, and oil rigs. They are not fussy predators, but they will not chase bait very far, so it's important for anglers to fish in extremely tight. Amberjack are schooling fish, and though this varies a bit by size (smaller fish are more likely to school up) once an angler hooks one, they are likely to hook many others.

More than anything else, the amberjack is known for its unparalleled, legendary fight. Other heroic fighters such as marlin, sailfish, and tarpon, are acrobatic and there is a beauty to their fight—it's an awe-inspiring combination of runs and jumps. Amberjacks aren't anything like that. They are brawlers, unbelievably powerful, and single minded. The reef donkey has one goal when hooked: get back into the structure and break you off—and they go hard. Particularly in the first minute of the fight, pulling a big amberjack out of a reef takes a titanic effort. This is not hyperbole: it takes everything the angler has, and even then, the fish still often wins. If you don't get the fish out immediately, it'll break you off, even if you're using a 200-pound (91 kg) leader. It's a heart-pounding, back-breaking, arm-burning, nerve-wracking few moments. Then, if the angler succeeds—which is a big "if"—the amberjack fights with an unmatched doggedness, using every molecule of its muscle for the entirety of the rest of the fight. All this to say, setting up on big amberjacks is not for the faint of heart and requires an all-out commitment by the angler—no hesitation, and no surrender.

The fight may be heroic, but targeting and hooking amberjack is straightforward. Dropping large live baits down to the fish on heavy conventional tackle is the most popular method. The key is to make sure the bait gets close enough to the structure that the amberjack will come out and grab it, without it getting hung up. This is even more difficult—but arguably more fun—when jigging. Anglers send large bucktail, knife, and metal jigs down deep, fishing very close and vertically over the structure, and then jig them aggressively up and down to draw attention. Getting slammed by a big amberjack as the jig falls, and then setting the hook and going all out to winch it away from the structure is an adrenaline rush that is hard to beat. Anglers often must get themselves psyched up before taking on this challenge, and it's common for them to stretch, take some deep breaths, and prepare themselves mentally before sending the jig down. For amberjack junkies, there is nothing like their beloved reef donkeys, and for certain, the fight of these savage fish is in a league of its own.

# HALIBUT

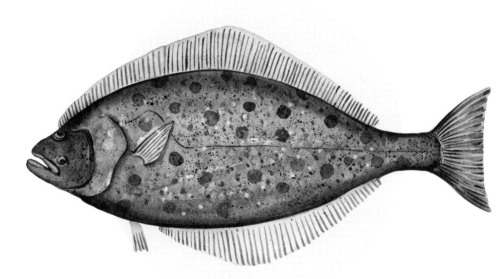

| | |
|---|---|
| | **· ATLANTIC AND PACIFIC HALIBUT: 300 POUNDS (136 KG) ·** |
| **DIFFICULTY** | **TROPHY SIZE** |

| | |
|---|---|
| **PERFECT SPOT** | Homer, Alaska, United States; Finnmark, Norway |
| **PREFERRED HABITAT** | Species dependent, but trophy-sized Atlantic and Pacific halibut live in deep subarctic waters, between 30 and 50°F (-1 and 10°C) and prefer soft bottoms in places with good tidal movement. They will associate with humps and bottom contour. |
| **SEASON** | Late spring and later through most of autumn are generally best for northern halibut species (Atlantic and Pacific), but it is highly location and species dependent. |
| **TOP TECHNIQUE** | The most consistent way to catch halibut is with bait fished very deep on heavy gear. This may require help from a guide. In some regions of the world halibut can be caught in shallower waters and with lures—fly fishermen even catch California halibut from the beach along the West Coast of the United States. |
| **AVERAGE SIZE** | Atlantic and Pacific halibut: 25 to 150 pounds (11 to 68 kg) |
| **RECORD SIZE LOCATION & DATE** | Atlantic halibut: 418 pounds 13 ounces (190 kg); Vannaya Troms, Norway, 2004 Pacific halibut: 459 pounds (208 kg); Dutch Harbor, Alaska, United States, 1996 |

## HALIBUT LOOK EXACTLY LIKE FLOUNDER—THEY HAVE THE

same flat and broad body, the same brown and patterned camouflage, upper side and milky-white blind side, and the same migration of their eye to one side of their body. Without any context, you would think they were the same fish—until you saw how big halibut get. The Atlantic and Pacific halibut in particular are some of the largest bony fish in the ocean, topping the scales at at least 700 pounds (318 kg).

Angling for giant halibut is generally not for the faint of heart. While smaller California halibut can be caught in more tepid conditions, they are the exception. Atlantic and Pacific halibut live in the frigid subarctic waters of the world, where the weather can be brutally cold. While anglers avoid rough seas for safety's sake, they sometimes need to take lengthy runs and cover a lot of ground to find the fish. This is followed by long bouts of jigging, or sending down heavy baits, often in heavy current, while the boat continually rocks and pitches. This can leave an angler bone-weary, with very cold hands and sore arms even if they don't hook anything. But once they do finally hook a halibut, fighting these big fish is a very physical task. The common nickname for large halibut is a "barn door," and dragging one up 500-plus feet (152 m) from the bottom can feel just like that. Only these barn doors can run, and hunt for bottom, and often when they see the boat, they will plummet all the way back to the bottom against the toughest gear and strongest drags—making the angler repeat the whole process again.

Most anglers around the world fish for halibut using bait they send deep, deep down to the bottom, fishing over humps and in areas of current. Baits vary, but herring, mackerel, octopus, and salmon all work well, and when you're hunting a giant halibut, often using an entire fish can be productive. Tangling with these fish involves very heavy gear, giant circle hooks, and sinkers the size of small barbells. While halibut will rise off the bottom more aggressively than many suspect, you still typically need to be down in the lower water column—and if you're fishing in 800 hundred feet (244 m) of water, you still may need to get down 600 feet (183 m)! It's nothing for anglers to use lead weights more than 3 pounds (1.4 kg) when fishing for halibut. There are also plenty of anglers that fish with lures. Jigs and big swimbaits are the most popular, especially when fishing in water that is relatively shallow—under 200 feet (61 m) deep—and when targeting "smaller" fish—under a couple hundred pounds.

While it's true they're primarily found offshore and in very deep water, halibut can be very flexible in their ability to thrive in a variety of environments. Like the flounder, they are voracious hunters and will pursue bait schools into the shallows. If the water temperature is between 30 and 45°F (-1 and 7°C), anglers can catch halibut in mere feet of water during specific phases of the season. And lest you think this means only baby-sized fish, anglers from California to Alaska in the United States and Vestland to Troms og Finnmark in Norway catch halibut that weigh hundreds of pounds in water as shallow as 20 feet (6 m) deep, even from shore and in kayaks. Catching these fish is a real adrenaline high, and the weight of a 200- or 300-pound (91 to 137 kg) halibut on the end of a line makes the heart race. For anglers who live in some of the coldest parts of the world, they are the premier sport fish that takes extreme levels of dedication, determination, and exploration to consistently land. The fact they are caught in some of the most pristine waters of the world adds to the allure and infatuation anglers feel for these massive fish.

# MAHI-MAHI

| | |
|---|---|
|  | **· 30 POUNDS (14 KG) ·** |
| **DIFFICULTY** | **TROPHY SIZE** |

| | |
|---|---|
| **PERFECT SPOT** | Offshore waters of the Bahamas and Panama |
| **PREFERRED HABITAT** | Mahi can be found in most temperate, subtropical, and tropical waters of the world with an optimum water temperature of 70 to 85°F (21 to 29°C). They are a pelagic fish that typically associates with floating vegetation, debris, and offshore structure. |
| **SEASON** | Mahi can be caught year-round. |
| **TOP TECHNIQUE** | Live and dead bait is almost guaranteed to get you a hookup once you find mahi. However, many anglers prefer casting lures that they retrieve very quickly, or throwing poppers that make a lot of noise on the surface. |
| **AVERAGE SIZE** | 5 to 15 pounds (2.3 to 7 kg) |
| **RECORD SIZE LOCATION & DATE** | 87 pounds (39 kg);<br>Papagayo Gulf, Costa Rica |

## THE MAHI-MAHI IS AN AMAZING FISH WITH MANY

outstanding traits, and it all starts with how they look. They are a uniquely proportioned fish, very thin straight on, with a blunt, flat face and a body that tapers from their blocky head to a deeply forked, large tail. Running along the top of their body is a long, sail-like crest that can be lowered or raised in response to the fish's attitude—they raise it when they're being hostile or aggressive. Their proportions alone would set them apart, but their coloring is the real stand out. A mahi's crest is deep blue, bordering on black, with an iridescent sheen. The upper portion of their backs is a bright, fresh-grass green that fades into a dazzlingly bright sunshine-yellow. Speckling of bright blue spots runs down their flanks, as if they were sprayed with paint. To say they are an unmistakable fish is an understatement.

The mahi—or dorado, dolphin, or dolphinfish as it is also commonly known—is a very athletic fish. The mahi is a real ripper, an open-water rocket, and once hooked they will jump over and over, skipping across the surface, and burning off drag. They can hit speeds of nearly 40 miles per hour (64 km/h) and use every ounce of that speed in their fights. The biggest mahi are often referred to as "bulls," and fighting one can feel like you're riding one in a rodeo. Plenty of anglers who count mahi as one of their favorite fish, and the all-out, take-no-prisoners fight is often why. Just the mention of them often brings a bright, beaming smile to an angler's face.

Mahi are pack hunters that can be found just about anywhere in temperate, subtropical, and tropical waters across the globe. They make incredible journeys and cover massive distances—they can swim more than 1,000 miles (1,609 km) in just a single month. Yet, the most incredible thing about mahi is their lifespan. They are one of the fastest growing fish, reaching 4 feet (1.2 m) long in 18 months, and they breed prolifically. Most don't live past 2 or 3 years, and mahi are ready to spawn in as little as 4 months, with females producing over 50,000 eggs each time they spawn—which can be 3 times a year. The combination of their early maturation, shockingly fast growth rate, and high egg count means mahi are one of the most common fish around the world.

A truly pelagic fish, anglers hunt for mahi in and around open ocean currents, often far offshore. Mats of floating vegetation and debris are synonymous with mahi fishing. Mahi use it for cover from predators, as hiding places to ambush prey, and as a nursery for spawning. If you are looking for mahi, this is the first place to start. Mahi can be fussy, but trolling and casting live or dead bait is highly productive in turning fish "on." Once the school gets fired up, they will attack voraciously. Anglers have caught them on virtually every lure and fly that exists, but the key is often going very fast or being very loud. One of the most reliable methods is casting and retrieving a tin, epoxy, or jig lure as fast as you can spin the reel handle; you can't go too fast for a mahi. Mahi also will blast poppers out of the water repeatedly, until they finally grab hold, and rocket off in a blistering, savage run—always punctuated by multiple jumps. The action can be fast, furious and a heck of a lot of fun.

The mighty mahi is a world-class sportfish—the really big ones are absolute bruisers, with endurance that puts most other fish to shame. Hunting those exceptional bulls is a game of meticulous planning, detail-oriented gear choices, and identifying solid patterns as to when and where the giants will appear. Many, many anglers love mahi, but the most devoted bull mahi-obsessed are rare—they are fanatics who are counted among the most talented anglers anywhere in the world.

# SAILFISH

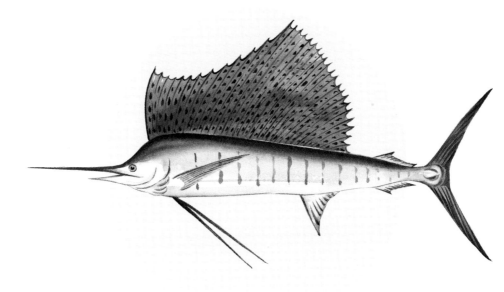

| | |
|---|---|
| **PERFECT SPOT** | South China Sea, Malaysia; Southeast Coast Florida, United States |
| **PREFERRED HABITAT** | Sailfish can be found throughout tropical and subtropical waters with an optimum temperature of 72 to 82°F (22 to 28°C), both near and offshore. They feed near the surface and follow baitfish and tidal currents. |
| **SEASON** | Caught year-round, depending on location |
| **TOP TECHNIQUE** | Trolling for sailfish is common, but the most fun way to catch them is sight casting bait or lures to feeding fish— lures that mimic baitfish are key. |
| **AVERAGE SIZE** | 30 to 100 pounds (14 to 45 kg) |
| **RECORD SIZE LOCATION & DATE** | 221 pounds (100 kg); Santa Cruz Island, Ecuador, 1947 |

## SAILFISH MAY BE ONE OF THE SMALLEST BILLFISH, BUT THEY

are the most athletic. It's generally accepted that sailfish are the fastest fish in the ocean, and they're able to reach speeds of over 60 miles an hour (96 km/h). This is faster than marlin, swordfish, or tuna, and the vast majority of land animals. They reach these speeds when hooked in the blink of an eye, can cover 100 yards (91 m) in 6 seconds, and be over the horizon before an angler can even react. Yet even this speed is not what makes the sailfish so astoundingly fun to catch—it's how much they jump and go all out on the surface. Sailfish have a knack for flying across the surface for long distances at full tilt, half-in and half-out, shaking furiously and spraying water like a mini cyclone.

Sailfish, as their name suggests, have a huge pectoral fin that they can raise or lower like a sail. It's several times as tall as their long, lean bodies. It's starkly dark blue, approaching nearly black, in contrast to their silvery bodies. This tall, long fin likely has multiple uses, including slowing the sailfish down from maximum speed when chasing prey. That said, most biologists and anglers agree that they primarily use it to corral bait and push it into tightly packed schools called bait balls—so named because the bait fish move in a tightly formed sphere. Once the bait is packed together, the sailfish can cut through it with its bill, stunning and injuring it. Then, it can circle back once more with its mouth open, inhaling multiple baitfish at once.

Even with their raucous fight and blazing speed, sailfish are less intimidating to catch than swordfish or marlin, and as such they are more accessible to any angler who wants to start pursuing billfish. They are small enough they don't require specialized tackle or ultra-long, punishing battles. On heavy spinning gear the sailfish is a formidable adversary, but the battle will be measured in minutes, not hours. They also don't require complicated lure systems such as marlin or dropping baits down thousands of feet like swordfish. Instead, catching sailfish is a lot more like fishing for many inshore species near the surface, where they spend most of their time. Sailfish also can be caught relatively close to shore, and in many parts of the world, they can be pursued with small center consoles, not massive yachts. Many anglers troll for sailfish with dredge lures, but it's also not necessary—learning areas that generally attract fish allows anglers to cast bait or lures to visibly feeding fish. Sailfish even make an amazing fly-fishing target, since they can be sight casted to on the surface.

For all these reasons, the sailfish is a billfish anglers revere with a deep and intense fixation. Plenty of anglers care only to catch sailfish, to the exclusion of all other species—even the giant marlin. And lest it sound like sailfish are pushovers for beginners, let that myth be dispelled; they are big enough, and fight in such a heroic manner that they can handily defeat the angler even if they're experienced and do everything right. They also can be extremely fussy and finicky to get to bite—more so than other billfish—and will reject unnatural baits a frustrating number of times. Further, they are also constantly on the move, and can travel many thousands of miles in their lives—keeping track of where and when they're going to be in specific areas takes meticulous planning. And like so many other fish, small sailfish may be a challenge, but trophy-sized fish take exceptional, total commitment and years of hard work to find, hook, and land with consistency. So, while average sailfish may be a stepping stone into the immense world of pelagic fishing for some anglers, trophy sailfish are the final destination for some of the most dedicated. They are by many measures the perfect sport species, mixing the best characteristics of so many other species into one beautiful, powerful, and dynamic fish.

# SWORDFISH

| | |
|---|---|
| **DIFFICULTY** | **· 500 POUNDS (227 KG) ·**<br>**TROPHY SIZE** |

| | |
|---|---|
| **PERFECT SPOT** | Gulf of Maine, United States; Bass Strait, Australia |
| **PREFERRED HABITAT** | Swordfish are deep water, pelagic fish. While they can occasionally be spotted on the surface, they hunt at depths exceeding 1,000 feet (305 m) in the world's temperate and tropical oceans with an optimum water temperature of 65 to 75°F (18 to 24°C). |
| **SEASON** | Swordfish can be caught year-round in most oceans where current temperatures remain constant. |
| **TOP TECHNIQUE** | Deep-dropping bait is the go-to for swordfish. Using squid is the best, as it's a staple of the swordfish's diet; many anglers employ small lights on their lines to attract the fish. |
| **AVERAGE SIZE** | 20 to 100 pounds (9 to 45 kg) |
| **RECORD SIZE LOCATION & DATE** | 1,182 pounds (536 kg);<br>Iquique, Chile, 1953 |

## SWORDFISH ARE A MYSTERIOUS, EXTREMELY CHALLENGING

fish that range the deep waters of the world's temperate and tropical oceans. They are proportioned like other bill fish—with heavily shouldered bodies and a massive, forked tail—and can match the marlin's weight, topping out near 1,500 pounds (680 kg). They are silvery gray with a dark dorsal side and a prominent, shark-like dorsal fin. Their namesake is their hallmark, which is a thick, broad sword at the end of their nose they use to stun prey and defend themselves against sharks and other open ocean predators. Their eyes are massive and represent a very unique attribute of these extraordinary fish. While swordfish do not keep their body temperature above that of the cold ocean depths like tuna do, they specifically heat their eyes. Warm eyes and nerves help them see light exceptionally well in dark, deep waters, but it's more than that—it also helps them hunt by increasing their ability to detect movement. Swords see at a faster rate than most other fish, increasing their ability to track prey, and pounce on it before the prey even realizes it's there.

Like marlin or wahoo, these are not fish for beginner anglers, and there are a lot of hurdles to jump in order to even hook one. The trickiest and most demanding part is just finding these fish, which are pelagic and almost always hunting in the wide-open ocean and often at depths in excess of 2,000 feet (610 m). They are always on the move, covering many, many miles in just a couple days. This means finding fish on one particular trip doesn't always yield fish on the next foray out to sea—they can simply disappear. They are also most successfully targeted at night, when they come up shallower (though this is relative). Daytime fishing has become increasingly popular but is still considered a marginal aspect of fishing for swords. As you might imagine, night fishing for 1,000 pound (454 g) fish, hundreds of miles out to sea and hundreds of feet down presents all sorts of additional challenges, and it is not for the faint of heart.

Modern marine electronics have made finding them easier, but even with the latest technology, tracking down swordfish can sometimes feel like trying to fish on the surface of the moon. The open ocean canyons are vast and mostly devoid of life, and the world at the bottom of the ocean is about as alien as you can get here on Earth. Anglers focus on ocean temperature gradients and tidal currents to help cut down on the search area, but even this leaves an immense area to cover. Then, getting the bait down the hundreds or thousands of feet to where the fish are feeding presents yet another logistical challenge. It's a lot of work moving the bait up and down with 8, 10, or even 15 pounds (4, 5, or even 7 kg) of lead on the line, and it's not something that can be changed quickly. For this reason, many anglers employ electric reels, which help get baits up and down quickly, while also allowing the angler to rapidly adjust their depth in smaller increments, and more regularly check their baits without getting exhausted.

Then, there are the battles with trophy swordfish on conventional tackle. These are hard to express in words, and there are few other fish that so aptly define the very word "epic." On stand-up gear, anglers have been forced to fight swordfish for an entire day or more—quite literally over 24 hours—and typical fights with giants are almost always over 6 hours. They are known to take 1,000 feet (305 m) of line in a single run, even towing along pounds of lead weight and against 30 pounds (14 kg) of drag and can pull a boat around for miles. They are shockingly fast for a fish that hunts in waters only a few degrees above freezing, but they also are bulldoggish and unrelenting. It's even amazing how much and how high they'll jump when they finally do hit the surface.

Swordfish are also mean, aggressive fish with serious attitudes and a deadly reputation. It's a brutal world down in the depths of the ocean, and the swordfish has adapted to be equally tough and savage. They are often covered in scars from battles with other swordfish, giant squid, mako sharks, and other denizens of the deep. On those rare occasions they are near the surface, they are known to charge right at divers and anglers who get in the water to hunt or film them. Fishermen and -women have been killed by swords; these fish are notorious for watching and waiting placidly boat side for an angler to try and remove the hook, and then lashing out with their massive bill. Some anglers claim they even intentionally try to jump into the boat to attack the angler. They are not fish to ever be trusted.

The elusive nature of giant swordfish and their savagery and unrequited fighting prowess puts them high in the hierarchy of gamefish. They're such a hard fish to find, hook, and land that they can quickly become a compulsion that nags at an angler day and night—it's all that comes to matter. The most dedicated swordfish anglers are few in number, but are some of the most knowledgeable, hardened, and dedicated across any species. There are few fish that require so much preparation and meticulous observation, as well as sheer determination and literal physical endurance to land. While many anglers will occasionally seek out smaller swords or attempt to land one or two giants in their life as part of a "bucket list," it takes a special kind of angler to dedicate themselves to trophy swordfishing season after season. Maturity, fortitude, and strength of will are not words used often to describe fishermen and -women, but these are precisely the traits required for any angler serious about the pursuit of trophy swordfish in the deep water, offshore canyons of the world's oceans.

With so many logistical hurdles to get over with swordfish, virtually all anglers use live bait. When you're sending your offering down so deep (which takes upward of 15 pounds, or 7 kg, of sinking weight), trying to entice and hook a fish on a lure is as close to impossible as you can get in angling. It's simply best to let the scent of the bait do the work in attracting and getting the fish to bite. To this point, anglers often use lights to attract swords from even farther distances. They will clip small flashers to their line at set intervals. These replicate the flashing of some of the swords' prey, like squid, and there is no doubt they make a huge difference in some locations. The actual bait preparation for swords is substantial, and anglers obsess over it. They will take strips of their favorite fish and sew in all kinds of other bits of flesh from different species. For example, a captain might sew freshly caught tuna flesh and a whole squid together with thick rigging thread to create a scent that is irresistible for the sword. They'll top this off with a rubber skirt that helps keep it together and give the visual illusion of a squid. All this preparation and the physical sewing together of the bait also prevents the sword—or other creatures of the deep—from pulling it all apart when they strike. The last thing you want to worry about is having to check your bait every hit when it's 2,000 feet (610 m) down at the bottom.

# WAHOO

| | |
|---|---|
| **PERFECT SPOT** | The Commonwealth of the Bahamas; Republic of Fiji |
| **PREFERRED HABITAT** | Wahoo are pelagic fish that can be found suspended over deep structure near drop-offs and warm ocean currents with an optimum water temperature of 70 to 80°F (21 to 27°C). |
| **SEASON** | Wahoo are year-round in many popular locations but are highly migratory and can travel more than 1,500 miles (2,414 km) in 6 months. |
| **TOP TECHNIQUE** | Virtually all wahoo anglers troll for wahoo with deep-diving swimming lures made for high-speed applications. Wahoo specialists prefer to troll between 10 and 15 miles per hour (16 and 24 km/h), but there are times they may go slower or faster, depending on a variety of factors. |
| **AVERAGE SIZE** | 20 to 50 pounds (9 to 23 kg) |
| **RECORD SIZE LOCATION & DATE** | 184 pounds (83 kg); Cabo San Lucas, Mexico, 2006 |

## WAHOO ARE OPEN OCEAN ROGUES FOUND ACROSS THE GLOBE.

They are very long and slender, with a tail-fork that's almost vertical and a head that ends in a very pointed nose, like a ballpoint pen. Their flanks are polished silver—very much like a tuna—with a navy blue dorsal side and dramatic dark blue or black vertical bands. They have no prominent dorsal fin, but instead a low frill that runs along their back. Most of the time, the fin is down, and this gives the wahoo—or "hoo"—the look of a stealth missile, an apt metaphor that perfectly describes their personality.

Wahoo are a big fish, and some of the fastest fish in the sea. These long-and-lean 100-pound (45 kg) fish hang motionless over deep structure and near open ocean currents, waiting for anything to venture too close. When still, they are disconcerting in their frozen state—like sleeping machines—but it's part of their camouflage in blending into the endless open sea. Then, when a bait fish gets too close, they instantly explode after prey in a devastating pursuit in which nothing can escape. When hooked, they have been recorded running at 50 miles per hour (80 km/h) or more, redefining the term "drag sizzler."

Speed is only the first part of what makes the hoo so deadly—the weaponry in their mouth is the second part. The edges of their jaws are lined with a perfectly straight row of small, arrowhead-like teeth that are as sharp as a surgical scalpel. To add more ferocity, a hoo's jaw closes with a crossing edge, where the upper jaw passes by the bottom, and doesn't come together like the jaws of most fish (or other animals). When the jaw snaps shut, it's like the closing blades of scissors. A hoo can cut right through a fish with a single chomp—and through 300-pound (136 kg) monofilament in the blink of an eye. The top jaw also hinges open at such a dramatic angle that a hoo can grab bait larger than its head and slice it in half instantly.

Wahoo require years of dedication to land with any consistency. There are a few reasons for this, and it all starts with the fact that they are widely scattered over huge areas. This requires covering lots of water in a single trip, often hundreds of miles in a day. They also live in deep waters, most often being caught between 100 and 300 feet (30 and 91 m) deep, but it is not uncommon to catch them in water over 1,000 feet (305 m). Getting a lure down to the hoo is the key to consistently hooking up, and trolling deep lures is the most common method. This is done at extraordinary speed—sometimes over 20 miles per hour (32 km/h)—requiring specialized lures and gear for success. The ultra-fast trolling triggers the hoo's impulse to attack, and they have no problem giving chase over long distances at these speeds.

The hoo also has a reputation as a dangerous fish for anglers. Once on the deck, a thrashing and snapping wahoo is a sledgehammer, knocking anglers off their feet and slashing ankles and legs with their teeth. Fishermen and -women have been known to lose toes and be sent to the hospital with large slices up and down their legs. Even after a hoo has bled out and in the cooler, they're still hazardous—inexperienced anglers have been sent to the hospital with serious wounds, just by accidentally touching the teeth of a dead wahoo.

Their elusive, dangerous, and brutal personality, along with the extreme methods required to catch them, make wahoo the favorite fish of many offshore anglers around the world. Searching for years in areas that consistently produce wahoo leads to a supreme sense of self-satisfaction for anglers who finally discover and lock onto a productive pattern. Then, after zigzagging over huge expanses of blue water at 20 miles an hour (32 km/h) with giant deep-diving lures, the rush of hooking fish that takes ridiculously fast, blistering runs against heavy conventional tackle is profoundly addicting. There is no fishing quite like it, just like there is also no fish quite like the wahoo.

# YELLOWFIN TUNA

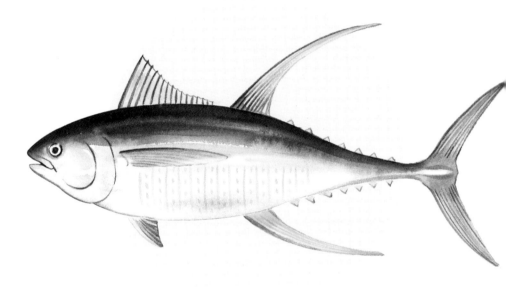

| | |
|---|---|
| **DIFFICULTY** | **· 250 POUNDS (113 KG) ·** |
| | **TROPHY SIZE** |

| | |
|---|---|
| **PERFECT SPOT** | Venice, Louisiana, United States; Oahu, Hawaii, United States |
| **PREFERRED HABITAT** | Yellowfin are found throughout the world's subtropical and tropical oceans but will push north into temperate seas with an optimum water temperature between 70 and 80°F (21 to 27°C). They are an open ocean fish, and follow bait schools, but can be found around deepwater humps and shelves. |
| **SEASON** | Finding yellowfin is about tracking their migrations and watching the water temperature. |
| **TOP TECHNIQUE** | Nothing beats throwing lures to yellowfin visibly feeding on bait. Poppers are great, but don't pass over subsurface presentations like soft plastics on a jig head or swimming stick baits. |
| **AVERAGE SIZE** | 20 to 100 pounds (9 to 45 kg) |
| **RECORD SIZE LOCATION & DATE** | 427 pounds (194 kg); Cabo San Lucas, Mexico, 2012 |

# YELLOWFIN TUNA ARE QUINTESSENTIAL TUNA, WITH A

sunshine twist. They are thick and tall-bodied, shaped like a rhombus, with a very large and forked tail, just like the other tuna in the world's oceans. The major difference (particularly between bluefin and yellowfin) is a set of long, bright yellow fins that sprout from their backs and bellies. This gives them a dramatic and exotic look. They have large eyes and excellent eyesight (for a fish), using their vision to hunt bait anywhere from 3,000 feet (914 m) down to right on the surface. In a debate over the hardest fighting fish, inevitably the yellowfin gets eclipsed by their gigantic cousin, the bluefin. Bluefin tuna grow so huge, it's hard for the much smaller yellowfin—which maxes out around 500 pounds (227 kg)—to compete. However, many anglers will fiercely defend the yellowtail as the hardest fighting fish on Earth, pound for pound.

As with many other tunas, their impressive bulk of muscle is powered by a countercurrent circulatory system that keeps their bodies warm, no matter the water temperature, allowing them to chase their prey almost anywhere. Yellowfin use their power and speed to cover thousands of miles in a single year, hunting various baits and spawning in a variety of different locations. While the yellowfin doesn't always venture as far north as the bluefin—it's primarily found in subtropical and tropical waters—they essentially go wherever food is most plentiful. Their size, speed, and warm bodies allow them to be boundless, and they cross the hemisphere repeatedly.

As the sun rises red and golden in the east, the sight of a school of yellowfin corralling and chasing bait to the surface, as birds fall from the sky like missiles, can stop an angler's heart; it's a beautiful, violent display of power by these voracious fish. Yellowfin tuna amass in exceptionally large schools that can provide anglers with an assault of the fiercest action imaginable. Their slightly smaller size—when compared to bluefin—makes them more fun to catch for most anglers. Instead of burning out from a single fish, anglers can hook and fight multiple fish, chasing the chaos from one bait ball to the next, all day. If you're looking for fast action over maximum size, the yellowfin is the obvious choice over the bluefin.

This is why the yellowfin is so beloved. Particularly in the Pacific where they get a bit bigger, they strike the perfect balance between being big enough to be very challenging on inshore tackle, but not so demanding they are "one and done." Like with so many other species within this book, anglers will hunt not just for the fish, but for productive yellowfin spots and seasonal patterns. Reeling in the fish is important, but identifying when the bite will be hot, and where the fish will be, can be even more meaningful. Once the angler identifies a few good patterns, the anticipation of a good bite becomes increasingly thrilling. Knowing the right weather and tides are about to align to produce dozens of 50-pound (23 kg) fish can keep an angler up at night, for days in advance. It's the kind of intense hopefulness that inspires childlike excitement.

Yellowfin tuna can be caught in a variety of ways, but like the bluefin, catching them on casted lures is a level of "intense" that is hard to match in the angling world. The lures utilized vary by location and time of year, but include poppers, stick baits, and soft plastics. It's important that the angler makes sure their hooks are extremely strong and sharp, even if they only anticipate tangling with smaller 15- to 40-pound (7 to 18 kg) yellowfin. These fish are strong and fast enough that top shelf, forged and stainless hooks are a requirement, despite the relatively diminutive size of the fish. Don't make the mistake of thinking a 25-pound (11 kg) yellowfin is the same as striped bass or halibut of the same weight—they most certainly are not. Yellowfin are high-octane pelagics that will punish any weakness in your tackle, no matter their size.

# EPILOGUE

# THERE IS NOW MORE PRESSURE ON OUR NATURAL RESOURCES

than ever before. As human population increases, our fisheries and waterways must contend with more and more use from both anglers and non-anglers alike. While it's always been important to consider your impact on the fish you're trying to catch and the environment in which they live, it has grown to be an essential part of being a conscientious sportsman or -woman. We all must unite in protecting our fisheries and waters—and preserving the pastime we are most passionate about.

Many fish in this book are delicious and healthy to eat. For many anglers, harvesting fish is an integral part of the fishing experience. It connects them to the natural world and gives them a deeper sense of ownership and stewardship of the resource. Preparing a meal for loved ones from fish you worked hard to catch can feel particularly satisfying. Where and when legal, there is certainly nothing wrong with taking a fish for the table when fish stocks are healthy and properly managed. However, I would urge you to learn about the fish you are harvesting. Even when legal, it isn't always in the best interest of a fishery for anglers to keep what they catch—especially if they fish a lot and keep fish every trip. Many fisheries are in decline, and we must all balance our individual desires to keep one for the table with the impact we collectively have on fish populations. I am not advocating you keep none—instead, I simply ask that you inform yourself on the status of the fish you are harvesting and make a responsible decision each time you head out.

A much larger concern of mine—and of many other sportsmen and -women today—is the way fish are treated that are going to be released. Taking steps to ensure all fish that are not going to be kept are let go healthy and strong is extremely important. It's far more important than most anglers realize. Release mortality—which is when a fish dies after it is released—is a leading cause of fishery decline across all types of water and species. Even if a fish swims away, if it is handled improperly, it very well may die out of sight of the angler. There are many ways to make sure you are limiting release mortality, but I would recommend a few as both the most important, and easiest, to implement.

First, make sure you're using gear that is adequately matched to the size of the fish you're catching. Long, protracted fights with gear that is too light can kill fish unnecessarily. I would also urge you to consider crimping barbs and using single hooks and circle hooks instead of treble hooks and J hooks whenever possible. These measures mean fewer fish are hooked in the gut, gills, or eyes—all injuries that can be fatal. Supporting fish under the belly—and not holding the fish dangling from the mouth—is something I've personally committed myself to more recently. Holding a heavy fish by the jaw can injure its mouth and spine, and even internal organs. It's been an adjustment for me that I'm still working on, but there is never a bad time to start, and no effort is wasted. We must adapt as we learn about new, best practices.

Finally, one of the most damaging mistakes you can make is keeping a fish out of the water for long periods. Frankly, this is probably the single largest factor in release mortality for all fish, across the board, and the worst thing you can do as a catch-and-release angler. For some fish, thirty seconds out of the water is no issue. For others, it can mean certain death. The best course of action is to simply release your fish as quickly as possible and keep them wet for as much of the unhooking process as you can. This, by itself, can have a significant impact. In the social media age we live in, getting a photo often comes first, and the health of the fish second. A photo can lead to extra-long periods of the fish being out of the water. Even as a professional writer and photographer—whose livelihood is sometimes predicated on getting "the shot"—I always think about the fish first. Getting it back into the water quickly is my number one priority; I can always get a photo next time.

We also must think about the water the fish we catch live in and the land around it. How we treat, preserve, and protect our natural resources is paramount to good fishing. This, of course, includes small things such as picking up trash, not leaving old line, bait, and hooks behind (which also is a number one culprit in losing access). But I think it's more than that. If you love it, prove it by protecting it. As a sportsman, I appreciate what it is that I have—the fish, the water, and the land—and treat it like it is a part of me. I believe, deeply, you should, too. Getting involved in preserving your natural resources has never been easier—many local and national groups do great work. These groups work with local anglers to maintain their waters in their natural, pristine state as well as protecting access and public land ownership.

Healthy and clean waterways have the most bait, the most fish, and the best fishing—this is an undeniable fact. I believe that their stewardship is up to us who love it most. If we wait for someone else to care about and protect our favorite lakes, rivers, or tidal habitats and the fish within them, that moment will never come. We will only see them continue to get used up and fade away: the dreaded shifting baseline. Now, more than ever before, it's up to us—the anglers—to be leaders and to care for our fisheries and natural resources as much as we care about catching the fish within them.

# RESOURCES

## IF YOU WANT TO LEARN MORE ABOUT ANGLING RECORDS—

and how you can beat them—check out the International Game Fish Association (IGFA). This historic group has been tracking records since 1939 and is a great resource for learning about the wider world of angling, too. **igfa.org**

If you want to learn more about fishing, there are many excellent magazines out there that can help take your fishing to the next level. Here are a few of my favorite publications to get you started: *In Fisherman* (**in-fisherman.com**), *Saltwater Sportsman* (**saltwatersportsman.com**), *Angler's Journal* (**anglersjournal.com**), and *The FlyFish Journal* (**theflyfishjournal.com**).

If you are interested in getting more involved with fishing conservation or learning about the status of your local fisheries, these are a few national organizations that have extensive information on fish species and their habitat and how best to protect it:

**Trout Unlimited:** This national nonprofit is one of the largest groups "conserving, protecting and restoring America's coldwater fisheries and watersheds." They are one of the very best fisheries conservation groups, and a powerful voice advocating for angler rights, including public lands access. **tu.org**

**Backcountry Hunters and Anglers:** BHA is a public lands advocacy group that has fought tirelessly to protect public lands for anglers and hunters. They have also weighed in on many conservation issues, including protecting fish stocks, habitat, and forage species. **backcountryhunters.org**

**Theodore Roosevelt Conservation Partnership:** The TRCP is a national group whose mission is to guarantee all Americans have quality places to hunt and fish. They advocate for funding for public lands, and fight for fisheries conservation across a broad range of issues. **trcp.com**

**U.S. Fish and Wildlife Service:** This is the only agency in the federal government whose primary responsibility is the conservation of fish, wildlife, plants and their habitats. They are an excellent resource for information on your local fisheries and they even have some great information to get you started if you've never fished before. **fws.gov**

**NOAA Fisheries:** NOAA Fisheries is responsible for the stewardship of the nation's saltwater resources—both fish and habitat. They have a lot of information on saltwater species, and even some tips on where and how you can catch them. **fisheries.noaa.gov**

**State Agencies:** Many states and regions have their own agencies that work to protect and manage fish species and their habitats. These agencies and divisions are often fantastic resources of information, including how to get involved locally.

While these national and state level organizations are all important, I would encourage you to investigate what resources are available to you at the local level. Many species have their own groups or clubs that work to preserve the species, educate anglers, and connect like-minded outdoorsmen and -women.

# ACKNOWLEDGMENTS

There are many who have helped support my writing, but I need to thank a few specific people who had direct impacts on getting this book published.

Thank you to Dave Anderson for publishing my very first article and photos, as well as your feedback and support throughout the years—you helped set me on this path. Along the same lines, thank you to Bill Sisson for helping me take my writing and photos to the next level and encouraging me to stay at it. I also want to thank Peter Jenkins for giving me my first seminar presentation opportunities and supporting my writing at every stage. Further, thank you to Zeno Hromin and Tommy Corrigan for trusting me with Surfcaster's Journal—your belief in me has meant a lot, and a lot of my writing skill was honed through the magazine. To John Skinner, thank you for telling me to "write what you know" and giving me the confidence to go for it, and write my own way.

I certainly also need to thank my editor Nicole James at Quarto for finding me and giving me this opportunity. Your patience with me at the beginning was deeply appreciated, and your input at every stage was essential in making this book as good as it is. Thanks for giving me a shot!

Thank you so very much to my aunt, Jo Ann Ferguson, for answering my millions of questions about writing a book, and helping me figure out how I was going to make this happen—you were instrumental in this achievement, and I'm not sure where I'd be without your guidance.

This book would not have been possible without the significant input from Toby Lapinski. Your insights, opinions, and advice helped me make many tough choices in this process and get over some substantial hurdles. When I needed someone to talk to about the book, you were the first phone call every time.

Thank you for also supporting me throughout my entire writing career—there is just no way I'd be where I am now without meeting you along the way. You are a truly great friend.

My passion for fishing would be nothing without my grandfather, Nelson Brown, and hence neither would my writing. Pop, those days on the trout streams changed my life forever. They were the fire that set my heart ablaze; you were the first person to show me what passion for fishing really was. It's the greatest gift I can possibly imagine receiving from anyone, and it's become a deep part of me, and will be forever. I can never repay you for it, but I hope you see how you helped forge my life's path.

Finally, words do no justice for the appreciation I have for my amazing wife Carly Audet. Carly, you are the greatest thing that has ever happened to me, and I'm perpetually in awe of your support and patience. I simply wouldn't have been able to do this without you. My writing—or really my whole crazy fishing life—is only possible because I know you have my back. Thank you for listening to me through all the highs and lows in this process, and being there when I needed advice, to vent, or just a hug. I would be lost without you; I wouldn't be the person I am without you. I love you, forever!

# ABOUT THE AUTHOR

Jerry Audet is a full-time freelance writer, photographer, and editor. He is a lifelong fisherman, general adventurer, and is well known for his dedication to surf fishing and fly fishing. Jerry's work has been widely published in the very best fishing periodicals including *Angler's Journal*, *Field and Stream*, *The Fisherman Magazine*, *On the Water*, *SaltWater Sportsman*, *Surfcaster's Journal* and more. He's had hundreds of his photos published in these publications—including many covers—and his photos (and words) have also been featured in several books by other authors. He also has an advanced biomedical degree and has published numerous works in the field of physiology. In addition to his freelance work, he is the managing editor of *Surfcaster's Journal*, a columnist for *Fishing Tackle Retailer*, the host of Surf Scenarios seminar series, and the cohost of *The Surfcast Podcast*.